Focus on the 90's:
Economics at Home,
Turmoil Abroad

THE M. L. SEIDMAN MEMORIAL
TOWN HALL LECTURE SERIES

RHODES COLLEGE
MEMPHIS, TENNESSEE

The M.L. Seidman Memorial
Town Hall Lecture Series

The M.L. Seidman Memorial Town Hall Lecture Series was estab-lished by P.K. Seidman in memory of his brother, M.L. Seidman, founder of the firm BDO/Seidman, Certified Public Accountants. Publication of this Twenty-Sixth Series of Seidman Lectures was made possible by a gift from Mr. P.K. Seidman to Rhodes College.

1967   *Financial Policies in Transition*
       edited by Dr. Thomas O. Depperschmidt

1968   *The USSR in Today's World*
       edited by Dr. Festus Justin Viser

1969   *The News Media-A Service and a Force*
       edited by Dr. Festus Justin Viser

1970   *Taxation-Dollars and Sense*
       edited by Dr. Festus Justin Viser

1971   *The University in Transition*
       edited by Dr. Festus Justin Viser

1972   *China's Open Wall*
       edited by Dr. Festus Justin Viser

1973   *Crime and Justice*
       edited by Dr. Festus Justin Viser

1974   *The Social Conscience of Business*
       edited by Dr. Phineas J. Sparer

1975   *The World Today*
       edited by Dr. Phineas J. Sparer

1976   *America: Heritage & Horizons*
       edited by Dr. Phineas J. Sparer

1977   *Big Government-Myth or Might?*
       edited by Dr. Phineas J. Sparer

1978	*The Middle East Crisis* edited by Mr. Peter W. Flexner
1979	*Education Daze* edited by Mr. William Thomas, Mr. Marvin Bailey
1980	*The Economy: Three Views* edited by Dr. Robert M. Cooper
1981	*Sports: Win, Place, or Show* edited by Dr. Robert M. Cooper
1982	*Management and Labor: Must They Be Adversaries?* edited by Dr. Robert M. Cooper
1983	*World Statesmanship and Trade: Help or Hokum?* edited by Dr. Robert M. Cooper
1984	*The Changing Job Market* edited by Dr. Robert M. Cooper
1985	*Dateline, The World* edited by Dr. Robert M. Cooper
1986	*Dateline, The World II* edited by Mel G. Grinspan
1987	*News and Views from National Public Radio* edited by Mel G. Grinspan
1988	*Ethics: Another Endangered Species?* edited by Mel G. Grinspan
1989	*Revolutions in World Economies:* *Their Impact on America* edited by Mel G. Grinspan
1990	*Evolution and Revolutions: The World in Change* edited by Mel. G. Grinspan
1991	*The Most Significant Events of the Past 25 years* edited by Mel G. Grinspan
1992	*Focus on the 90's: Economics at Home, Turmoil Abroad* edited by Mel G. Grinspan

Library of Congress Cataloging-in-Publication Data
Focus on the 90's: economics at home, turmoil abroad.
    p. cm.–(M.L. Seidman memorial town hall lecture series; 26)
    Lectures delivered Feb.-Apr. 1992 by Dr. Andrew Michta, L. William
Seidman, and Georgie Anne Geyer
    1. Post-communism 2. Savings and loan failures–United States. 3. Savings
and Loan Bailout. 1989-   I. Michta, Andrew, A. II. Seidman, Lewis William,
1921- . III. Geyer, Georgia Anne, 1935- . IV. Series.
HX44.5.F63   1992
330.9'049–dc20   92-17018
                                                            CIP

Focus on the 90's:
Economics at Home,
Turmoil Abroad

edited by Mel G. Grinspan

RHODES COLLEGE
MEMPHIS, TENNESSEE

1992

COMMUNITY ADVISORY COMMITTEE

DUNBAR ABSTON
Business Consultant, Teacher

WALTER P. ARMSTRONG, JR.
Attorney, Armstrong, Allen, Prewitt, Gentry, Johnson and Holmes

ROBERT BUCKMAN
President, Chief Executive Officer, Buckman Laboratories

MARCIA CONDO
Trustee, P.K. Seidman Foundation

DAVID HARLOW
Executive Vice-President, Rhodes College

DR. JAMES HOLBERT
M.D., Ph.D., M.B.A., Chief of Hematology, Baptist Hospitals

DR. CECIL HUMPHREYS
Ph.D., President Emeritus, Memphis State University

DR. JAMES HUNT
M.D., Chancellor, University of Tennessee Health Science Center

LIONEL LINDER
Executive Editor, Memphis Commercial Appeal

HARRY PHILLIPS, JR.
Chief Executive Officer, Browning Ferris- Industries

MILTON C. PICARD
Attorney, Picard & Caywood

P.K. SEIDMAN
Tax Attorney

RHODES COLLEGE COMMITTEE

HELEN NORMAN
Assistant to the President for Public Information

LOYD TEMPLETON, JR.
Assistant to the President for College Relations

SALLY PALMER THOMASON
Dean, Meeman Center for Special Studies

MEL G. GRINSPAN
Series Director, Distinguished Service Professor Emeritus
Adjunct, Meeman Center for Special Studies

Contents

Introduction   i

Lecture Number One   1
Dr. Andrew Michta
Holder of the Mertie Willigar Buckman Chair
of International Studies, Rhodes College
    Introduction by
    Mel G. Grinspan
    Distinguished Service Professor Emeritus
    Lecture Series Director
    Rhodes College

Lecture Number Two   62
L. William Seidman
Former Chairman,
Federal Deposit Insurance Corporation
    Introduction by
    Winton M. Blount
    Chairman of Board, Blount, Inc.
    Chairman of Board, Rhodes College

Lecture Number Three   95
Georgie Anne Geyer
Columnist, Broadcaster, Educator
    Introduction by
    Dr. Andrew Michta
    Holder of Mertie Willigar Buckman Chair
    of International Studies, Rhodes College

Focus on the 90's:
Economics at Home,
Turmoil Abroad

An ongoing challenge to the administration of the M.L. Seidman Town Hall Lecture Series is the creation of themes based on the most topical and provocative subjects, to secure lecturers who are recognized and respected authorities on the chosen topics, and to do so within the limits of the resources available to the Series. This makes the process even more of a challenge, one that is more daring today than in the earlier days of the Series. In our modern world of instant communication, there are few matters with any degree of public interest which are not brought to the public's attention immediately and repeatedly. To give that news increased credibility, expert opinions are sought and aired or printed. The result is a proliferation of information on the broadest variety of subject-matter by increasing numbers of recognized authorities. Today, one need only to punch a button or turn a dial to see and hear experts on a multitude of subjects.

How, then, does one account for the continuing success of such programs as this lecture series? Why, since its inception in 1966 when the airwaves and the print media were not so loaded with personalities, facts, fiction and opinion, has this Series been continuously successful in attracting so many to its programs? The excellent caliber of the lecturers is a prime factor and, of course, the theme of each year's series is meticulously chosen for topicality and interest. But, there is strong empirical evidence that much of the answer lies in the town hall aspect of the Series which encourages the audience to warm up to the lecturer, to ask pointed questions, to get immediate answers and, most of all, to feel the lecturer's actual presence. The lecture hall takes on an air of expectation as the lecturers take the podium and deliver their messages, but the atmosphere becomes electric as the audience and the lecturer join in the provocative question and answer period.

This abiding human touch was never better demonstrated than during the 1992 Series, "Focus on the 90's: Economics at Home, Turmoil Abroad". Our lecturers were Dr. Andrew Michta, holder of the Mertie W. Buckman Chair of International Studies at Rhodes College; L. William Seidman, former Chairman of the Federal Deposit Insurance Corporation; and, Georgie Anne Geyer, a featured international affairs columnist and broadcaster. In each case, the capacity audiences favored the lecturers with a wide variety of questions, all of which were answered graciously and with the funds of knowledge each exhibits so effectively. The questions and answers for each lecture are included in this volume.

The '93 Series was opened by Dr. Michta whose subject matter was the plight of eastern Europe and the former Soviet Union in the '90s. He presented an in-depth analysis of each region of the vast territory which was part of the former Soviet Union, as well as each member of the newly-founded Commonwealth of Independent States and other erstwhile members of the Soviet bloc. As he vividly described the present state of these old and yet strikingly new entities, he also pondered their prospects for the balance of this decade. The picture Dr. Michta paints is a drab one at the best. The multitude of human, cultural, religious and political problems facing the new nations as they thrash their ways to something resembling free-market economies could prove to be overwhelming. Those that do not succeed could find themselves chained again to a returned command state, perhaps not communist as we have known it, but certainly as binding and restrictive as before the replacement of the totalitarian regimes.

Dr. Michta emphatically connected the welfare of the western powers with that of the new and re-emerging nations of eastern Europe. He strongly feels that western long-term interests are at risk if the post-communist states do not succeed in their struggles for democracy and market economies. Fact is, Dr. Michta was amongst those international voices calling for substantial US and other western aid long before President Bush, seemingly prodded by political pressure, decided to seek the 24 billion dollar aid package to the CIS he now feels is so imperative. Michta has believed this aid to be essential in order to maintain the degree of stability that is necessary if the Eastern European nations involved are to survive the immediate future. He has advocated the urgency for humanitarian aid as well as quick access to technological aid to help the people of those beseiged nations sense at least a modicum of confidence as they experience their bleak present and wonder about their questionable future. A short time after Dr. Michta emphasized the absolute necessity for massive aid in his lecture, the International Monetary Fund publicized the findings of a study estimating that to stay afloat the CIS would require 44 billion dollars in aid the first year and in excess of 140 billion dollars over a four year period. But even in the face of such outside financial and technological aid, the situation is a precarious one because the fledgling nations still must contend with profound internal problems which, if not solved or ameliorated, could result in "an explosion of popular discontent".

Dr. Michta brought his audience up-to-date on a rapidly changing and important part of the world. Running through his presentation was the disturbing reminder that the freedom flood that began in Tiananmen Square,felled the Berlin Wall and surged on to the multifaceted soil of Eastern Europe and the USSR, has left in its wake a multitude of complex problems, many quite obvious, others yet to assert themselves.

Though Georgie Anne Geyer's lecture did not follow Dr. Michta's in sequence (her's was preceded by L. William Seidman's), her presentation is being considered here because she discussed the same part of the world as Dr. Michta, but in a completely different context. While Dr. Michta dwelled on the historical, geo-political, and economic aspects of the region, Ms. Geyer introduced us to some of the beset people who must contend each day with the macro problems discussed by Dr. Michta.

Ms. Geyer's style is uniquely engaging. She talks the way she writes...with the same warmth, earnestness and genuine interest. She forms a bond with her reader or listener, one that stays glued because her sincerity and knowledge are so strong. She interprets the intimidatingly vast problems of today's world into human terms and discusses their effects on the individual and parses them down to their most understandable components. And she accentuates her unique approach by "going through hell and high water", if necessary, to reach the places and the people for the material she seeks, whether they are heads of state or the least known member of a remote village someplace in Central America.

A strong sense of this Geyerian penetration to the soul of a story was felt by her audience as she described her experiences in what was once the Soviet Union. She asks what happened to the once-formidable empire. Why did it happen so quickly? We have witnessed the collapse of an entire governmental system without war while watching with wonder as the people of the system seemingly clamor for the idealogy —democracy — of their former enemies. There are others who dwell on the obvious problems confronting the people in the face of such drastic changes, the economic, cultural and social transformations which are inevitable. But Ms. Geyer wonders about the profound psychological problems of humiliation which tear at the very fibers of human beings whose world as they have known it turns upside down before their very eyes. Simply stated, she says that the overwhelming majority of the people of the former Soviet Union don't know what to do, and those who do know don't know how to do it.

In her travels throughout the former Soviet Union, Ms. Geyer spoke at length with people in all walks of life, from community and political leaders to ordinary citizens grasping for some kind of meaning to what was happening to them and their villages and cities. She describes in graphic detail the conditions existing in these various settings and paints vividly her impressions of people and their surroundings. Then, toward the end, she admonishes Americans, representing another way of life both physically and philosophically, not to lose the sense of values that has made them the leading exponents of those principles which so much of the rest of the world is struggling to embrace.

L. William Seidman was our second lecturer. He is former Chairman of both the Federal Deposit Insurance Corporation and of the much-discussed Resolution Trust Corporation, the body created to dispose of the defaulted savings and loans associations. Mr. Seidman has a vested interest in the Series. He is the nephew both of the man who the Series honors, M.L. Seidman, and the man who established the Series, P.K. Seidman. He is also the son of Frank E. Seidman for whom the internationally recognized award in political economy is named and which also is administered by Rhodes College.

Bill Seidman, as he is best known, has a wealthy background of experience and insight in the workings of government on the state and federal levels. The excellent reputation he has built over the years stems not only from the expertise he has developed in the areas of his service and from his understanding of their political underpinnings. He is also known for his penchant to "tell it the way it is" and to do so simply and to the point. That is precisely what he did as he discussed the outlook for the US financial system.

Beginning with a brief history of the 1980's incursion into crooked maneuverings by some of the country's better known financial wizards, Mr. Seidman walked his audience through the mess that was wrought and the results that followed. Special attention was paid to the savings and loan associations. When their life-threatening ailment was finally diagnosed, Mr. Seidman explains that, though the treatment and medication may have made the patient feel better in the short run, over the longer period, the illness was only exacerbated and infected many parts of the banking and thrift industries. The basis for the dire treatment prescribed was deregulation, the prescription so widely proclaimed by the Reagan administration and, of course, the patient was helped little by the uncooperative Democratic Congress.

But even in the face of his tale of despair, Mr. Seidman assures us that the prognosis for the financial health of the country is positive. There are promising signs in such factors as inflation, debt-load, oil prices and interest rates. As for when we can expect to see definitive signs of a recovery from the recession, he suggests that it will take place "just in time to save the Bush presidency". Mr. Seidman is bullish about the future, too. He points to major changes poised to improve industry in general including the banking and financial sectors . Then there is the growing potential of such "unregulated" financial services as the asset-based lenders GE, AT&T Capital, Household Finance and many others.

Mr. Seidman ended his lecture with his optimistic view of the US future in worldwide competition, but he qualified it with several hard caveats, not the least of which is to stop emphasizing today in our planning and start giving proper thought to tomorrow.

The 1992 Series was highlighted by large, attentive audiences who lingered long after the lectures were over to further the discussions or just to chat with the lecturers. It was another indication of the continuing effectiveness and popularity of such programs as this Series which is made possible through the generosity of Mr. P.K. Seidman to whom we at Rhodes College are most grateful.

I also extend a special thanks to Angela Walker for her help in the preparation of this volume.

Mel G. Grinspan
Lecture Series Director
Distinguished Service Professor Emeritus,
Rhodes College

Focus on the 90's:
Economics at Home, Turmoil Abroad

Introduction of

Dr. Andrew Michta

by Mel G. Grinspan
Distinguished Service Professor
Emeritus, Lecture Series Director

I believe there are very few of us who have not heard or seen tonight's lecturer either on TV, on radio, or in the newspapers. Since coming to Rhodes in 1988, Professor Andrew Michta has gained national and international recognition in the field he will discuss with us tonight. Professor Michta holds the Mertie Willigar Buckman Chair in International Studies here at Rhodes College. And we are very proud that members of the Buckman family who established the Chair are with us tonight.

Professor Michta received his doctorate in International Relations at Johns Hopkins University after receiving a Master of Arts Degree in American Studies at Michigan State University and his Bachelor of Arts degree at St. Mary's College in Michigan.

Prior to coming to Rhodes, Professor Michta was a John M. Olin Fellow and Visiting Scholar at the world-renown Hoover Institution on War, Revolution and Peace at Stanford University. He also was deeply engaged in effective research work in the private sector where he was the author and editor of various important studies on Soviet politics, economics, defense, science and technology. So you see, our lecturer tonight, who has made many fact-finding and fact-giving trips to that part of the world and has conferred with the power people in Eastern Europe and what was the Soviet Union, is especially well-qualified to discuss that area of the world with us tonight. But there is an added ingredient to Professor Michta's qualifications... a vital one that makes understanding a country, a people and its culture in an unique and especially meaningful way. Professor Michta speaks Russian and Polish fluently, not to mention his ability to speak French and Italian.

It's a genuine pleasure for me to now call on Professor Andrew Michta.

Focus on the 90's:
Economics at Home, Turmoil Abroad

Lecture Number One by

Dr. Andrew Michta
Holder of Mertie Willigar Buckman Chair,
International Studies, Rhodes College

Good evening ladies and gentleman. I am honored to be the first lecturer in this year's Seidman Lecture Series at Rhodes. Tonight I will focus on the politics of postcommunist reconstruction in what was once the powerful Soviet bloc. In my lecture I will review the emerging sub-regions of postcommunist Europe, I will discuss the continuing decomposition of the former Soviet Union, and I will suggest several possible directions of change in the postcommunist world during the remainder of this decade. First, I will review the current situation in three regions most important to the emerging new order in Europe: (1) the "Triangle" of Poland, Czechoslovakia, and Hungary, (2) the Balkan states, and (3) the two key Soviet successor states of Russia and Ukraine which are the principal members of the new Commonwealth of Independent States (formerly the USSR except for the Baltic states and Georgia). I will also address the issue of the Western, and more specifically, American response to the collapse of Soviet-style communism. Considering time constraints, this is a tall order indeed, but I hope that during the question-and-answer period we will be able to address in more depth those issues which are of particular interest to you.

Postcommunist Europe: Old Divides and New Divisions

The notions of the East and the West, both of which are quintessentially political and do not reflect the history or cultural divisions of Europe, were at the center of the world order of the past four decades. As one observer put it[1], the great "civil war within the Western world, which began with the Great War of 1914, carried us through the horrors of World War II, and then into the stalemate of the Cold War," has finally come to an end, With the challenge of

Soviet communism no longer here, it is time to survey the "landscape after the battle" and to try to answer the question about the future of what used to be the Warsaw Pact. Indirectly, this is a question about the much debated new "world order" and America's place in it.

Let me first make several general observations which will serve as a context of the discussion. Eastern Europe has had a unique place in the history of the 20th century. Two world wars that devastated the Continent and exploded the Euro-centric international order originated in Eastern Europe. Furthermore, after 1945 the Cold War was joined because of the Soviet-American confrontation over Eastern and Central Europe; in turn, the Cold War ended in 1989 in a dramatic "autumn of the peoples of Eastern Europe," which set in motion the revolution that ultimately brought down the communist empire. For close to half a century, between 1945 and 1991, Eastern Europe constituted the frontline in the confrontation between two mutually exclusive visions of the social and economic world order. During that time, changes in East European politics were both influenced by and were a reflection of the superpower relationship. Control over Eastern Europe was critical to the Soviet Union's claim to superpower status, for it meant the emasculation of German power. The 1949 creation of the German Democratic Republic was symbolic of Russia's true historic gain from World War II; conversely, the German reunification in October of 1990 meant in effect Russia's defeat and the failure of its bid for global leadership.

Today what used to be Eastern Europe of the Cold War era is rapidly fragmenting along a new north-south divide, reflecting changes in the distribution of economic power and political influence on the Continent as a whole. The emerging new Europe is becoming increasingly centered around its developed northwestern core, in particular Germany, with the areas lying southeast of the center progressively losing their relative importance to Europe's politics. At the same time, this north-south fragmentation of Europe is being accompanied by the reintegration of Europe's northwestern core. In 1985 the European Community made the decision to bring about economic and political unification in the year 1992. This is 1992, and although the new conditions of post-communist Europe have raised the stakes considerably, Europe's general commitment to unification remains, with the goal of widening the EC to include less developed European countries clearly gaining the upper hand. The European Community has already decided on the following two stages of integration, to include first the European Free Trade Association states (Scandinavia, Austria, and Switzerland), and next the Triangle, that is Poland, Czechoslovakia, and Hungary as the second-tier new members.

Among former Soviet bloc nations of what once was communist Eastern Europe, the so-called "Triangle" of Poland, Czechoslovakia, and Hungary has good short-term prospects for integration with the developed West and for becoming the eastern periphery of the new Europe. On the other hand, Romania, Bulgaria, and the remnants of the defunct Yugoslav federation (with the possible exception of Slovenia and Croatia) find themselves increasingly outside the purview of European integration, as they are mired in ever more violent nationalism. As we move farther east to the territory of the former USSR the situation becomes even more complex. Despite the magnitude of economic problems at home, the three Baltic states have a fair chance of eventually integrating themselves with Europe via EFTA, specifically through the Scandinavian countries. The three remaining key Soviet successor states, that is Belarus, Ukraine, and Russia are only now beginning the painful first steps toward Europe; their success is far from assured. It depends on the outcome of the growing conflict between Russia and Ukraine, the two key CIS states, as well as on Russian President Boris Yeltsin's ability to maintain his core of popular base of support and the loyalty of his military.

Let me review in some detail the principle economic and political issues facing each of the post-communist countries, from the Triangle, through the Balkans, to Ukraine, and Russia.

The Triangle

Poland, Czechoslovakia, and Hungary, or the "Triangle" as the three have been called since the collapse of communism, are well on their way to become viable members of the new Europe. The three have demonstrated their determination to make the necessary adjustments, however painful they might be in the short run, to make them eventually full members of the EEC. On November 15, 1991, the Triangle became an associate member of the EEC, thus gaining the badly needed access to the Western European market for its agricultural and industrial products. While EC associate membership has not eliminated all barriers, it has dramatically improved the Triangle's prospects for successful economic reform.

Poland introduced its radical economic reform program in January of 1990. The Balcerowicz plan, named after the country's finance minister, has set its goal curbing inflation, adjusting prices to the world market level, making the currency convertible, and privatizing the state-owned industries. With the exception of the privatization program, it has been a dramatic success. Inflation has gone down from 1,100% in 1989 to 50% last year. The supply situation has radically improved with thousands of new businesses set up in the process. The Polish zloty is now internally fully convertible, with the "heavy zloty" to be introduced sometime this year. Unemployment is over one million, but so far the social safety net has been able to cope with it. Government subsidies in Poland today constitute less than 5% of the GNP. The one major failure in Poland has been the privatization program, because the government failed to muster the courage to undertake drastic measures bound to leave thousands of workers jobless.

Czechoslovakia began its own reform in January of 1991. It is a three year program of gradually transforming the country's economy into a market system. However, Czechoslovak reform has been hampered by the fear that it may lead to the disintegration of the federation itself. Since most of the country's heavy industry is located in Slovakia, including over a hundred defense plants, most of the unemployment will be Slovak. In light of strong separatist pressures in Slovakia (former Slovak Prime Minister Vladimir Meciar spoke of leaving the federation altogether), Prague has been very careful not to risk the confrontation. The goal of Havel's government is to shield Slovakia from suffering the brunt of reform.

Privatization in Czechoslovakia has centered so far on the sales of selected industrial plants to foreign investors, including the sale of the Skoda works to Volkswagen and the Skolunion glass factory to Glaverbel of Belgium. Most foreign investment in Czechoslovakia has come from Germany and Austria, raising concerns in the Czechoslovak foreign ministry about the country's future ability to make independent foreign policy decisions.

Hungary has been the most successful of the three in bringing about a rapid transformation to the market economy. Already in 1990, 50% of all foreign investment in Eastern Europe, including eastern Germany, went into Hungary.[2] By mid-1991 over 7500 new joint ventures were registered in Hungary. The country's new legislation, including 16 new laws that facilitate foreign investment and set up a credit system for Hungarian businessmen to acquire state-owned assets, has made Hungary an attractive target for investment from Europe, the United States, and Asia. In 1991 Budapest was the only Eastern European capital where two leading Japanese banks opened their branch offices. Budapest has also addressed the question of privatizing agriculture. On January 7, 1992, the Hungarian parliament approved a new law, which allows for the privatization of cooperatives in agriculture, industry and services, and which outlines the privatization procedures.[3]

Hungary has also been more successful than any other East European country in finding solutions to the devastating loss of the Eastern market in the wake of the implosion of the Soviet Union. In 1990 Hungary managed to increase its exports to the West almost as fast as its exports to the East were falling; in the first quarter of 1991 Hungary earned a $150 million current account surplus in its EC trade.[4]

In sum, despite the growing pains associated with the post-communist reconstruction, the Triangle is well-positioned to accelerate the process of its integration with the developed West.

The Balkans[*1]

Since the implosion of the Soviet bloc, the Balkan's have been increasingly living up to their reputation. In contrast to the relative success of political and economic reform among the Triangle states, they have been mired in nationalism. The disintegration of Yugoslavia in the wake of the Serbian-Croatian war has provided a

---

[*]I am excluding Albania, because since the 1960's the country has been effectively outside the Soviet bloc. While since 1990 political reform has been introduced in Albania, its outcome is marginal to the developments in the Balkans as a whole.

dramatic example of how complex and volatile the Balkans have become, now that the Cold War pressures are no longer there. Slovenia and Croatia have moved decisively to become fully independent states. In addition, the government of the Yugoslav Republic of Macedonia announced on the 27th of January, 1992, that it would create its national army[5]—the decision which in my view is the first step toward independence. Clearly, the Yugoslav federation belongs to the past.

Romania is still controlled by former communists. The Iliescu regime, which consists largely of the anti-Ceausescu group within the former Romanian communist party, has solidified its position following the 1990 free elections, which were notorious for the government manipulation of the process. The National Salvation Front government has remained authoritarian, suppressing the calls for greater democracy. The government's policies toward the opposition have been condemned by Western governments, including the United States which recalled its ambassador to Romania in protest over the 1990 electoral manipulation. Although some reform of the political system has taken place, including greater freedom of the press, Romania continues to be governed by the so–called Supreme Council for the Country's Defense whose members have been hand picked by President Ion Iliescu. The opposition has rightly compared the Supreme Council to the Politburo of the Romanian Communist party during the Ceausescu period.[6] The Supreme Council has become a vehicle for direct control by Iliescu of all ministries, thus effectively bypassing Romania's government.

Romania has remained isolated in the region, despite its efforts to build closer ties to the West. Its relations with Hungary are perfectly bad over the question of the Magyar minority in Transylvania, in Romania. The Hungarian government has openly accused Romania of engaging in the "cultural genocide" of the ethnic Hungarians. Romania reciprocated by charging Budapest with unacceptable interference in its internal affairs. Tension along the Romanian-Hungarian border has been so high that the two sides resorted to an "open-skies" agreement, which since the summer of 1991 provides for regular overflights of each other's border zone by the aircraft of the countries' air forces equipped by the French to detect troops and armor concentration on the ground. The overall goal of the agreement has been to lower the risk of an armed border conflict. Still, the "open skies" agreement notwithstanding, the relationship has continued to deteriorate. In late October of 1991 Erno Rudos, Hungarian Ambassador to Romania, described the Hungarian-Romanian relationship as "unsatisfactory."[7]

Bulgaria's progress toward democracy has proceeded slowly and haltingly. In late 1991, the country did hold free elections which finally pushed the Bulgarian Socialist Party (former Communists) out of power, but so far the new government has proved indecisive in dismantling the old economic system. On January 30, 1992, Bulgarian Prime Minister Filip Dimitrov announced that his government has decided to freeze prices on key consumer goods.[8] The Dimitrov cabinet is a coalition government put together under the umbrella of the Union of Democratic Forces. It is only beginning to draft the stabilization and privatization programs.[9] The reforms may be coming too late to save Bulgaria's economy from total collapse, despite the additional $200 million in credits made available by the EEC in 1991. The breakdown in the basic services in some parts of the country has raised the specter of a viral hepatitis epidemic. In the region of Gabrovo in central Bulgaria over 300 people have already contracted the disease because of poor sanitation and the general shortage of medicine. Considering the poor conditions throughout Bulgaria, the epidemic may spread quickly.

The Dimitrov government has displayed a desire to move closer to NATO as it welcomed the NATO Rome summit initiative in November 1991 that will provide for consultations with former Warsaw Pact countries. The Bulgarian foreign ministry announced that Zhelyu Zhelev, the country's president, will travel to Brussels to ask for closer ties with the Atlantic Alliance. It is unlikely, however, that the West will reciprocate, considering the internal conditions in Bulgaria and the country's only marginal importance to the European security system.

Today Bulgaria finds itself increasingly isolated from the core of Europe. To make matters worse, its relations with neighboring states are tense. Bulgarian-Turkish relations have been badly damaged by the decades of official discrimination against Bulgaria's Turkish minority, especially by the Todor Zhivkov communist government's forced "bulgarization" of entire Turkish villages in the mid-1980's, which at the time led to a mass exodus of Bulgarian Turks. Over the past decade, Bulgaria's relations with Romania have been growing increasingly tense because of Romania's disregard of the environmental impact of its Chemical Works in Giurgiu, in the Danube Valley, on Bulgaria's north, especially on the city of Ruse, Bulgaria's fourth largest urban area. Bulgaria has demanded that the Romanians close not only the Giurgiu plant, but also the Romanian Metal Works in Calarasi, which has systematically polluted the Bulgarian town of Silistra to the point that it is now virtually uninhabitable. In both cases, Bucharest responded with defiance, canceling the planned official visit to Bulgaria by Romania's minister of the environment.[10] In addition to its tense relations with Turkey and Romania, Bulgaria has reasons to be concerned over the direction of the Serbian-Croatian war in the former Yugoslav federation. Sofia has feared that if the war spreads it may reach Bulgaria's western border.

Russia, Ukraine, and the Commonwealth of Independent States

The Commonwealth of Independent States, which includes 11 former Soviet republics (with the exception of the three Baltic states and Georgia) is in my view a poorly-defined formula for holding the Soviet successor states together. It has been created as a last minute effort by the Soviet republics to find a common ground between the complete emancipation of the nations formerly controlled by Moscow and the reconstitution of a new federal union, as advocated by Gorbachev during his last year in office. As such, the CIS is likely to fail, for if the present centrifugal forces continue unchecked (in particular, the growing conflict between Russia and Ukraine) they will culminate in the creation of fully independent successor states. On the other hand, if Moscow decides to reassert control despite the opposition from the non-Russians, the CIS will move in the direction of a stronger centrally-controlled multinational federation under Russia's aegis. In either case, the Commonwealth formula as we know it today, i.e., as a loose confederation of the Soviet successor states led by Russia, is not likely to endure.

The CIS is supposed to provide for equality of its members, and yet Russia has insisted on retaining the ruble as the common currency, thus making it impossible for the non-Russian states to have an economic policy of their own. Russian President Boris Yeltsin has asserted that all CIS members are sovereign states, while also insisting that a unified army must be preserved and that all nuclear weapons must be transferred to Russian control. Russia remains the primary supplier of energy and natural resources to the CIS members, and thus it can exercise considerable pressure on the other states by threatening to deny them access to the vital raw materials. In short, the CIS formula as it is defined today clearly favors Russia. It requires that the non-Russian successor states give up voluntarily what Moscow held by force in the past: their independent statehood. Ukrainian President Leonid Kravchuk articulated the common consensus among the non-Russian CIS states when he accused Moscow of "imperialist tendencies." Kravchuk has made it abundantly clear that his country will guard its sovereignty regardless of the cost. For the non-Russians experiencing their first taste of independent statehood, the Commonwealth formula may be simply too little too late.

The former Soviet Union finds itself in a revolutionary situation, which makes it dangerously prone to either a military coup d'etat or the rise of an authoritarian government. The USSR has lost a war (in this case, the Cold War competition with the West), which for decades has sustained and partially legitimized the old communist regime and the Russian empire. The administrative institutions of the former USSR have collapsed, central controls have imploded, the economy has ground virtually to a halt and poverty is spreading at a rapid rate. In 1991, in 30 out of 70 territories in Russia, the death rate exceeded the birth rate. According to a TASS report of January 24, 1992, in 1991 the Russian population grew by only 0.2%[11]

During his six years in office, Mikhail Gorbachev effectively dismantled the mechanism of the Soviet state without replacing it with a new structure. As a result, the successor states are now desperately trying to restore a semblance of an orderly administration on their territory in the face of increasing chaos. In my view, two factors will be critical to the future of the Commonwealth: (1) the behavior of the CIS senior military and (2)

Yeltsin's ability to maintain his core support base in Russia while riding out the tide of popular discontent which has been rising as this winter progresses.

For the senior Russian military, the Commonwealth is the only assurance that the army will remain unified. Hence, the military has supported Yeltsin's efforts to preserve the new confederation as the heir to the Russian and Soviet empires, for the demise of the Commonwealth would mean the demise of the unified army. Conversely, however, if Yeltsin wavers in his commitment to preserve one army (and we see the signs of this in his acquiescence to the transfer of the portion of the Black Sea navy to Ukraine), the army may feel compelled to take over the government to prevent the Commonwealth from collapsing, and thus to preserve itself as an institution.

The current pressure from Ukraine has thrown open the question of the future of the combined armed forces, and has evoked an angry response from the CIS senior military. Today Marshal Evgeniy Shaposhnikov, the commander in chief of the CIS forces, is his own politician, accountable more to his fellow officers than to Yeltsin or Kravchuk. During the historic founding meeting of the eleven CIS states, on December 30, 1991, Shaposhnikov threatened to resign if the army were to be divided up by individual states.

The CIS army is beginning to challenge directly the authority of the civilian government. On January 15, the officers of the two paratrooper divisions still stationed in Lithuania issued an ultimatum to Yeltsin demanding social guarantees to their families upon return to Russia and threatening to ignore orders and to mutiny if the demands are not met. Yeltsin has been repeatedly attacked by his own vice president, who, as an air force general, appears to place his loyalty to the military above his constitutional obligations to Yeltsin. Vice President Rutskoi's attacks on Yeltsin's policies are an ominous warning of the prevalent mood among the officer corps. On January 17, five thousand officers of the All-Army Officers' Assembly, which met in Moscow to urge the retention of a unified army, demanded government action to preserve it and to improve the standard of living of the military. The meeting adopted a statement warning against attempts to divide up the army and created a council that will represent the military's interests in dealing with government. According to the poll taken at the time, 67% of the Assembly officers present insisted that one unified army must be preserved. In short, as the economic crisis deepens and the CIS continues to alter, the military may choose to mutiny to preserve the unity of the army.

The other key question is Yeltsin's ability to retain the core of popular support which made it possible for him to defy the failed August 1991 coup and to replace Gorbachev. Over the past several weeks, we have witnessed the progressive decline of the popularity of civilian authority throughout the Commonwealth. On January 14, 1992, Yeltsin, the man who only a month ago was hailed as the leader with a mandate for change, was confronted in St. Petersburg by angry residents demanding to know how they were going to feed their families. Similar sentiments have been manifest throughout the former USSR. On January 16 in Tashkent, the capital of Uzbekistan, six students were killed while demonstrating against the government's economic policies. On January 19, three thousand people marched in St. Petersburg against price liberalization and called for the resignation of Yeltsin and Mayor Anatoliy Sobchak. Protests are beginning to spread to other cities, including strikes by ambulance drivers in Yakutsk, teachers and students in Kaluga, and the threat by subway workers in St. Petersburg to close the entire subway system unless their wage demands are met. If the population reaches its endurance level, Yeltsin's popular support will crumble.

The rising wave of mass discontent has been reflected in the increasingly acrimonious squabbling among the presidents of the Commonwealth states. The relative decline of Yeltsin's popularity has been accompanied by growing friction among the governments of the successor states, in particular the conflict between Russia and Ukraine, the two key states of the new confederation. In January of 1992, the Ukrainian government refused to give up its claim on the army and navy units stationed on its territory, forcing a confrontation that has threatened to explode the new Commonwealth almost immediately upon its inception. Both Russia and Ukraine have made territorial claims on the Crimea, and the issue is likely to fester. The Ukrainians have repeatedly accused Russia of "imperial tendencies" and warned Moscow not to attempt to dictate policy within the Commonwealth. More importantly, Ukraine has reneged on its earlier pledge to transfer all nuclear weapons back to Russia.

In order to retain the core of popular support Yeltsin needs to be able to provide for the most basic needs of his people. Therefore, it is imperative that during this winter, food and energy supplies in Russia remain uninterrupted. This is the urgent message Yeltsin has been carrying to Western capitals during his recent trips to Europe and the United States, and he is clearly willing to trade a portion of Russia's nuclear arsenal for Western aid. During his recent visit to the West, Yeltsin promised to cut Russia's defense procurement by 50%, announced the elimination of 130 land based ICBMs, and promised to reduce Russia's defense budget by 10% this year.[12] He has also cut off temporarily the supply of oil and natural gas to Poland and Czechoslovakia, although under the current barter agreements Russia is obliged to continue sending oil and natural gas to the two countries. Yeltsin's primary goal is to ensure that Russia's energy supplies are sufficient to meet the domestic consumption needs of the CIS, because his own political survival depends on it.

Yeltsin's success, and in the final analysis the preservation of the CIS, rest on his ability to stabilize Russia's economy. The market stabilization plan, introduced in Russia in January of this year, is attempting to achieve macroeconomic stabilization, to curb inflation, to create the internally convertible ruble, and to privatize the economy. In its general outline, the plan is reminiscent of the Balcerowicz program adopted in Poland in January of 1990 (Jeffrey Sachs has been an adviser to both Balcerowicz and Yeltsin). However, important differences between Poland and Russia make the prospects for the plan's eventual success much more tenuous in Russia than in Poland.

The foremost obstacle to reform is the very scope of the task. There is a Russian saying which goes as follows: "Russia is not a country, Russia is a world." Even if one excludes the ten non-Russian states, the size of Russia itself makes such a wholesale transformation of its economy a herculean task. Next comes that basic nature of Stalin's economic blueprint which has turned the Soviet Union into one centrally controlled economy. Throughout the seventy-five years of the Soviet Union's existence the steel plants of Russia depended on the ore and coal extracted in the Ukraine; the chemical plants in the Baltic region depended on raw materials and energy supplies from the Russian republic; Russia's textile plants relied on cotton from Uzbekistan for their operation—in short, the Soviet industries, their raw material, their energy supplies, and their markets were spread out throughout the Eurasian landmass, with the central planners paying more attention to political considerations than to economic common sense. As a result, the newly-independent successor states are saddled with inefficient industries with the necessary raw materials and energy sources, and without the markets for their products. In general terms, we witness a situation similar to that faced in 1918 by the successor states to the Hapsburg empire.

Finally, there is the question of the values that seventy-five years of communist dictatorship have imparted in the people of the former Soviet Union. Democracy is only as good as the society that supports it. Russia, Ukraine, and the remaining CIS nations are only beginning to learn the fundamentals of self-government. Civil society in Russia is only beginning to emerge. It will take time before it is restored. If one looks at the devastation visited by communism on Ukrainian and Russian peasantry one will appreciate how difficult privatization of agriculture is bound to be. In my view, it will take a new generation before democracy has taken root in the former USSR. Therefore, the remainder of the decade will be critical to Russia's future.

Prospects for the Rest of the Decade

The process of post-communist transformation in what used to be the Soviet bloc is far from over, and the successor states face widely different prospects in their endeavor. The Triangle of Poland, Czechoslovakia, and Hungary is well positioned to complete the change, save for a global economic crisis that would undercut their still tenuous economic position. Since the reunification of Germany, the Triangle has been the de facto eastern periphery of the developed Europe. For the first time since 1949, Poland has a common border with a NATO member state. The three have expressed their commitment to become full members of the EC and to come as closely as possible to the North Atlantic Alliance. More importantly, witness the November, 1991 decision to grant the Triangle associate membership in the EEC. The developed European nations have responded favorably to these overtures, encouraging the Triangle to maintain its reform policies. It is reasonable to expect that by the end of the decade, Poland, Czechoslovakia, and Hungary will become full members of the EC, coming into the community as the "second wave" after the admission of the EFTA countries.

In addition, the Triangle states have been cooperating within the so-called Pentagonal/Hexagonal group, which includes in addition to Czechoslovakia, Hungary, and (as of July 1991) Poland, also Italy, Austria, and the now defunct Yugoslavia.** The group has relied on Italian and Austrian capital and technology, and on the Triangle's labor and natural resources to restore the infrastructure from the Danubian basin north to the Baltic sea. Currently the Pentagonal/Hexagonal group has over 100 projects under review, including building a north-south expressway to link the Baltic sea with the Adriatic sea, laying the fiber optic cable for the future modern telecommunication system, and cleaning up the environment.[13]

The situation looks much less promising in the Balkans. With the exception of Slovenia and Croatia, the Balkan states find themselves in the "other Europe," whose value is judged by the developed North as questionable at best, and whose economies and political institutions are not yet suitable for pan-European integration. While the Balkan states are members of the CSCE (the Conference has recently been enlarged to include the CIS republics, thus making the organization even less effective), they face no realistic prospects for becoming even associate members of the EC any time soon. To make matters worse, the fighting in the former Yugoslav federation in 1991-1992 may only be the beginning of a series of violent regional confrontations, in which the developed West will not intervene because its vital interests are not at stake as long as the violence remains limited. In short, the collapse of communism and the disappearance of the East-West divide of the Cold War has returned the Balkans to their peripheral status in Europe. The significant difference between their role today and, say before World War I or even during the Cold War, is that violence in the Balkans now lacks the larger pan-European and international dimension. Paradoxically, limited wars in the Balkan today appear tolerable for

---

**Slovenia and Croatia are likely to assume the responsibilities of the Yugoslav federation within the group.

they do not affect directly Europe's northwestern core and, in the absence of superpower competition, it does not threaten to escalate to a global conflict.

In contrast, developments in the former Soviet Union, especially in Russia, merit careful attention. The worst possible outcome of the present crisis would be the severance of ties between Russia and Europe. A Russia that is excluded from Europe will become isolated, difficult to deal with, a threat to its former clients, and a constant concern to Germany. The German government has demonstrated a remarkable appreciation of this basic reality of the post-Cold War European politics. Bonn has been the principal force behind the Western aid effort to the CIS. It has committed itself to assist the Russians in building housing for the troops being withdrawn from Europe and to the long-term effort to help Moscow to complete the transition to a modern-day market economy.

German policy has demonstrated an enlightened self-interest and an appreciation of Russia's potential in the next century. Russia has natural resources, which are tangible assets and which can serve as the necessary collateral for Western developmental aid. Furthermore, Russia's oil and natural gas resources constitute for Europe a viable alternative, especially in light of the continued volatility in the Middle East. This lesson was driven home during the gulf War crisis. Finally, chronic instability in the former Soviet Union would make it virtually impossible for Central Europe to complete the post-communist reconstruction. The prospect of having to deal with hostile neighbors in the East would no doubt scuttle the current prospects for successful economic and political trans-formation in the Triangle, thus leaving Germany (and hence the developed core of Europe) with perpetual instability on its border. In the event, such an outcome might be a compelling enough reason for Germany to rearm and to pursue policies increasingly independent of the Western community.

Western Policy Objectives

The danger faced by the post-communist states is one of continued instability, which may bring about the escalation of violence to unacceptable levels. Considering the large nuclear arsenal in the former USSR, the US and its NATO allies have a vital interest in preventing nuclear proliferation and the large-scale transfer of nuclear technology to the Third World. It must be stressed that the best solution to the post-communist nuclear dilemma is not the purchase of those weapons (as some Western experts have suggested), but the restoration of Russia as a member of the new European and global order. In effect, by assisting Russia in making an orderly transition to the market system and, consequently, to a stable democratic government the West will achieve the goal of effective control over the remaining nuclear weapons. The alternative, that is the breakdown of all order and the potential for the rise of Russian fascism or revolutionary Muslim states in place of the Central Asian republics is a dangerous and a real possibility.

In my view, short of a military coup or the rise of an authoritarian regime in Moscow, the progressive emancipation of the Soviet successor states will continue until they become truly sovereign nation-states. Whatever the outcome, it is in our interest to ensure that the process does not turn violent and uncontrollable. I am of the opinion that complete emancipation of the CIS states, especially Russia, Ukraine and Belarus, would be the preferred solution, because it would both reduce the degree of instability in the region and lay the groundwork for meaningful economic reform. While massive economic assistance to the CIS would in my view be wasted as long as the national question has remained unresolved and the economic reforms have not been firmly in place, the West can and should help by providing the necessary humanitarian aid and technical expertise to prevent an explosion of popular discontent.

Today the old image of the Soviet enemy belongs in history books. In absolute terms, Western security has improved exponentially. This, however, may prove a temporary situation if the post-communist reforms fail. Humanitarian considerations aside, the United States and Western Europe have a genuine long term national interest in assisting the postcommunist states in their effort.

Notes

1. William S. Lind, "Defending Western Culture," *Foreign Policy*, Fall, 1991.
2. "Hungary takes the lead on foreign investment," *The Financial Times*, May 14, 1991.
3. *RFE/RL Daily Report*, January 8, 1992.
4. "Hungary goes west with a new urgency," *The Financial Times*, May 2, 1991.
5. *RFE/RL Daily Report*, January 31, 1991.
6. This allegation was made by Victor Iancu in an article for the newspaper *Dreptatea*. See "Article Criticizes Defense Council's Power," *FBIS-EEU-91213*, November 4, 1991, p. 23.
7. "Hungarian Envoy: Bilateral Ties Unsatisfactory," *FBIS-EEU-91-212*, November 4, 1991, p. 23.
8. *RFE/RL Daily Report*, January 31, 1992.
9. "Dimitrov Presents Policies to National Assembly," *FBIS-EEU-91-218*, November 12, 1991, p. 5.
10. "Ruse Issue Further Mars Relations with Romania," *FBIS-EEU-91-217*, November 8, 1991, p.11.
11. *RFE/RL Daily Reports*, January 31, 1992.
12. *RFE/RL Daily Reports,* January 30, 1992.
13. Pentagonal Initiative: Program of Work (1990-1992), (Venice, August 1, 1990), pp. 1-11.

Questions and Answers following
DR. ANDREW A. MICHTA'S LECTURE

*Q: What have the Germans done in the zone of what used to be
Eastern Germany since West Germany's government used to play
an important role in the post-cold War Europe?*

A: The price tag of the reconstruction of Eastern Germany is
tremendous. I think that Chancellor Kohl has, in effect, under-
estimated the resources that must be invested in the former GDR.
Eastern Germany is now a part of the Federal Republic. It has been
restructured into five new states. The current migration from Eastern
Germany into West Germany is causing the depopulation of eastern
Germany. An interesting side development of this process is the
simultaneous migration of people from Poland, Czechoslovakia, and
Hungary into eastern Germany, concurrent with migration from
Russia into Poland, Czechoslovakia, and Hungary. This patten of
migration indicates that the conditions the migrants initially
encounter, as they move West, are dramatically better than those
they left behind.

As for Germany, it will take Bonn the entire decade, I think, to
bring the East up to the standard of the rest of the country. As it
continues to rebuild at home, Germany has a unique opportunity to
develop a new relationship with Russia. While on this subject, I
would like to add something about the German-Russian relationship.
Some observers have made comparisons between the current
German-Russian negotiations and the Rapallo Treaty of 1922,
suggesting that the coming together of the Germans and the Russians
is bound to make many West Europeans very nervous. I don't
believe this is the case. In fact, before the collapse of communism,
West Germany's trade with the East, that is not only with the former
Soviet Union but also with Eastern Europe, was never greater than
6.5% - 6.7% of the Federal Republic's total foreign trade.

Today, trade with the East is not a golden economic opportunity
when compared to Germany's economic prospects in trade with the
West. In short, the German opening to Russia is *par excellence*
political, that is, Germany wants to ensure that Russia remains

engaged in European affairs. I am afraid of what would happen to Russia if it were excluded from Europe. It would be a resentful and hostile Russia, and under such conditions, Germany would see no other alternative but eventual rearmament. If faced with this kind of volatile and hostile environment in the East, Germany would once again begin to refocus its attention away from the West. This, in turn, would endanger the integrity of the Western security system.

Finally, let me comment on the strains that reunification has placed on the German economy. The Germans are doing something that in the past four decades they considered unthinkable—they have opted to run up inflation by agreeing to convert the East German mark to Deutschmarks on a one-to-one basis because the political goal of bringing the East Germans into one state as quickly as possible has been paramount. It was a difficult decision for the German government to exchange the East German currency in that way. Since the 1950's the Germans have routinely opted for higher unemployment in order to keep inflation down. Let me add that the reunification of Germany has a global economic dimension in that it is putting additional pressures on the world capital markets today. In my view, it will be another 6 or 7 years before the process is completed. In effect, by the turn of the century, Germany will be in a position to play the kind of role it is destined to play in the European Community, a leadership role.

Q: In the EEC they are talking about having a common currency, the ECU, which is based on the Deutschmark. There is an ongoing debate in Great Britain in particular on whether this is such a great idea in regards to giving up its sovereignty and so forth. What do you think?

A: The British have long resisted the idea of a common European currency. I think the debate over the ECU has heated up in part because of what is going on in Germany. It was obvious that the European currency unit, when it was conceived, would be pegged to the Deutschmark. Today there is some concern that while the Germans are running up inflation, they will be effectively exporting this inflation to the other EEC countries. The argument is that if the common currency is introduced now, France, Great Britain, and other developed countries in the European Community will be in effect paying a portion of the price tag for the reconstruction of eastern Germany. This is in sharp contrast to the early 1980's when the Germans were pursuing virtually zero inflation policies and had a very strong currency which could pull the pound up; however, some in Great Britain now fear that the opposite may be true, and that this may not be the right time to introduce the ECU. I personally think that a common currency will be eventually introduced, and it matters less whether it is called the ECU or the Deutschmark, for that matter.

Let me now comment on the broader issue of European integration. I believe for the remainder of the decade we will see integration progress along the horizontal line, that is we will see the broadening of its scope to cover new members, rather than the deepening of integration within the existing EEC countries. The European Free Trade Association is expecting to enter the EEC by the middle of the decade. Next in line are the "Triangle" of Poland, Czechoslovakia, and Hungary. The horizontal extension of the EEC will also mean that for now the integration will be more limited than envisioned in 1985. This should not be surprising. It took the EEC quite some time to get to where it stands now. It is the most promising formula for European integration that we have.

I didn't mention the Conference of Security and Cooperation in Europe on purpose. The CSCE has been touted for some time as a kind of all-inclusive formula for the future; a pan-European security process that will ultimately bring the European countries together. As you know, the CSCE has been expanded to include all of the members of the new Commonwealth of Independent States, the successor to the Soviet Union. This makes for a rather peculiar situation, because the Central Asians are now part of the European security system. The net result is that the CSCE is now even less effective than before when it comes to providing collective security or settling disputes. Its ineffectiveness has been exposed in the context of the current Serbo-Croatian war, where the CSCE's role was quickly eclipsed by the EEC and the UN. In my view, the CSCE is useful as a forum for debate, but not as a working security framework for post-communist Europe.

In contrast to the CSCE, NATO is already in the process of

transformation, and if the trend continues it will come to undergrid the security system on the Continent. So far NATO's plans call for the creation of a rapid deployment of force to be run by the British (never the Germans, mind you), which should be able to move throughout Europe in case of an emergency. There is also a strong possibility that the 1949 Washington Treaty may be renegotiated to allow for the stationing of NATO troops on the territory of non-NATO countries. This would allow NATO to intervene militarily, if need be, in the most unstable regions of Europe.

Q: What is the United States position in this development other than to provide food and temporary help now? And how could we market democracy in that part of the world?

A: I think we are still extremely popular in the former Soviet bloc, including Russia. The United States is to the East Europeans the most powerful symbol of democracy. In Eastern Europe, Ronald Reagan remains unquestionably one of the most popular presidents in the history of the United States, and to the majority of the East Europeans we remain the political and economic model to aspire to. On the other hand, I don't think we can do very much in practical economic terms. The reasons are as follows: number one, we simply don't have the money to institute a "Marshall Plan for the East;" and number two, I don't think the political and economic situation in Russia and some of the East European countries is right for massive Western economic aid. We can, however, contribute to the region's stability by remaining engaged. We can do two things. Even though Germany is firmly anchored in Europe, and Russia is not the threat that it used to be, the majority of East Europeans want America to maintain its presence in Europe. The existence of NATO, with American presence, however symbolic and token, proves that the transatlantic connection is vital to Europe and that it will not be severed any time soon. This by itself calms a lot of fears in Eastern Europe and contributes to stability in the region. It is highly symbolic of how America's presence in Europe is viewed by the East European that the greatest objective of the Triangle has been membership in NATO. Even Boris Yeltsin said he would like Russia to join NATO. Whether or not this comes to pass depends on how

NATO changes and if it is capable of opening up to new members; however, it is undeniable that the role of the United States will continue to be very important as the key security anchor in a region.

The second point I want to make concerns American private investment which has an important role to play in the reconstruction of postcommunist Europe. With companies such as GE or GM investing in Hungary, or Levi's investing in Poland, American business can help the region recover, while at the same time transferring the badly needed technology and managerial skills to the East Europeans. Our government assistance to Eastern Europe is limited. We have a program which provides seed money to small businesses in Eastern Europe, but this is a limited program. Capital is not all. Eastern Europe needs Western technological expertise, Western advice and assistance in cleaning up the environment. Even such basic assistance as sending Peace Corps volunteer to Eastern Europe to teach English or basic accounting skill matters. I think with time these various efforts will add up to a critical mass that will accelerate post-communist transformation in the region. The most important assistance the United States can offer today is its continued presence in Europe as an implicit security guarantee to the new democracies.

Q: What are the prospects in Russia? How many are considering the gold standard to stabilize the ruble and if they did what effect would that have?

A: Russia has no more gold available at present for such a massive operation. In fact, one of the most incredible stories since the beginning of Gorbachev's era is that beginning in 1985 the Russians have been selling off their gold reserves to pay for imports. Their gold reserves are currently estimated at no more than $4 billion. So, although Russia's potential in terms of raw material deposits is tremendous, at present Russia doesn't really have the resources available to it. The Russians can have a convertible ruble but they have to do it the same way the Poles, the Czechoslovaks, and the Hungarians did it. That is, by freeing prices and allowing the currency to be adjusted in response to market forces. They are trying to do this, as you can see in Yeltsin's economic reform program. We know from the Polish example how it works. In the case of Poland a lot of private entrepreneurs jumped on the bandwagon once the reform was in place. All of a sudden, thousands of small businesses appeared overnight, people began to shuttle back and forth through Germany, Spain, and France bringing in goods, reselling them, and purchasing foreign currency because of the development of a currency market. It is true in that Poland has the advantage of its proximity to the West. Russia's problems are much more complex. As of yet, Russia lacks a private sector strong enough to provide the necessary competition. As a result, you still have state enterprises in the Russian system in a monopoly situation, and that distorts the markets. The managers of Russian plants have become essentially the owners, which means they can deal whatever they want and are not accountable to anyone. The Russians still can't deal effectively with agriculture either. Throughout the communist period, Poland had private farming, which— even though it was very inefficient— meant that the concept of private land ownership survived. In contrast, one of the most devastating problems for Russia is the fact that there aren't any private farmers left in the former Soviet Union. The people who knew what it meant to manage land were eliminated by Stalin in the 1930s as the so-called *kulaks*. Since then the people who worked on the collective farms in the former Soviet Union were essentially regular laborers, hired field hands who were paid a salary for their work but had little control over the fruits of their labor. It appears that today these people are not very interested, especially considering their history, in seizing the current opportunities to start privatization in agriculture. One comment on Russia's agriculture with reference to the food situation for this winter: the problem is not so much the shortage of food, but the breakdown of the distribution system in the country.

Q: The Wall Street Journal *recently reported that there are hundreds of thousands of warehouses controlled by the military. Is food coming in from the West and is it controlled by the politicians?*

A: I don't think it is a question of the politicians but rather the "Russian mafia" that has contributed to the frequent breakdowns in the food aid distribution system. Crime has become a large problem in the former Soviet Union, and the theft of Western aid ranks among the most immediate problems. The Germans have complained repeatedly that much of the food and medical aid that goes into the former Soviet Union have been stolen and resold for profit on the private market. In the end, the only way that the Russian government knew how to respond to this was to use the army to unload the airplanes bringing Western aid. In fact, the reason for using military facilities as temporary warehouses is to decrease the probability of theft. You probably have seen footage on television of Russian soldiers unloading and guarding Western cargo planes. These patrols were introduced because up to 50% of all of the available material aid (anything from formulas for children to disposable syringes) coming into Russia would disappear upon arrival, stolen from the warehouses by the well organized criminals. The administrative system in Russia is still corrupt, and it's not that difficult for the gangs to bribe government officials.

Q: I have two questions. How do you see the conflict between Czechoslovakia and Hungary over the minority issue resolved? And the second question is whether you see the idea of Slavic nationalism playing a role in the future of Eastern Europe and the Soviet Union?

A: The first question. The potential for conflict between Prague and Budapest over the ethnic question goes back to the post-World War I settlement. As a result of the breakup of the Austro-Hungarian Empire, a large Hungarian minority found itself outside the Hungarian state, among other states in Slovakia in the Czechoslovak federation. This made Hungary by definition a revisionist power. The largest Hungarian minority lives today in the Transylvania region of Romania; in addition, Hungarian ethnics live in Slovakia and in the Vojvodina region of former Yugoslavia. Tension between Prague and Budapest over the Hungarian minority rights has been a greatly publicized problem, especially after Hungarian Prime Minister Antall made a statement that he considers himself responsible for Hungarians living outside the country's territory. Prague, Bucharest, and Belgrade condemned the statement as unacceptable interference in the internal affairs of their countries. The Hungarian and Romanian governments have engaged in hostile and confrontational rhetoric on the minority issue and that bodes ill for the future of their relations. On the other hand, most of the differences on the minority issue between Hungary and Czechoslovakia are being negotiated, and good progress is being made. The real problem in Czechoslovakia is Slovak separatism. Vladimir Meciar, the former prime minister of the Slovak republic said that he wanted Slovakia to join the EEC under its own flag. Meciar is no longer Slovakia's prime minister, but the new Prime Minister Carnogursky also insists that Slovakia has a right to independent statehood. The history of animosity between the Czechs and the Slovaks reaches back to the interwar period. Slovakia has always been the less developed part of the federation. These are two different nations, even though Czech and Slovak are similar languages (if you understand one, you can understand the other). Similarly, the Czechs and the Slovaks have very different historical experiences. Slovakia had an experience more under the influence of Hungarian ethos, whereas the Bohemian and Moravian experience was more similar to the German culture.

The situation is not hopeless, though. A 1991 poll showed that 70% of the Slovaks are in favor of preserving the federation, provided that the federal constitution guarantees their rights and proper representation at the federal level. Still, the relationship between the Czechs and the Slovaks is a very tense one. For example, when the name of the country was being changed after the collapse of communism the federal parliament debated for weeks whether the country should be called the "Czech and Slovak Federal Republic," the "Czechoslovak Federal Republic," or the "CzechSlovak Federal Republic." At the time, heated arguments were joined in the Czechoslovak federal parliament over the size of the Slovak cross in the national emblem, whether or not the Slovak cross in the emblem should be the same size as the Czech lion, or bigger, or small, or should the Czech lion carry the Slovak cross on its chest, or should the cross be placed next to the lion? We can laugh at these things, but in the Czechoslovak context these are symbolic of how difficult the relationship between the Czech and the Slovaks is.

As for your second question, I don't think pan-Slavism or any notion of common Slavic national heritage can work in today's East

European context. In fact, we can see that it doesn't work in the Ukrainian-Russian relationship either. In fact, the CIS formula is a non-starter as far as the non-Russians of the former USSR are concerned because it is ultimately a prescription for continued Russian domination in the area. The Russians expect that, for example, the Ukrainians will give up voluntarily what the Russians took from them by force in the past, which is not a realistic expectation, to put it mildly. The entire region of the former Soviet bloc is full of nationalist hatred and unresolved territorial grievances. For example, there is a history of hatred, war, and atrocities committed by both sides between the Russians and the Ukrainians, or the Ukrainians and the Poles. These are all very, very difficult relationships. For instance, the Russians and the Ukrainians have a very real territorial dispute over who owns the Crimea. The Russians claim it's theirs; the Ukrainians claim it is theirs. Finally, the Ukrainians, especially in the western part of the country want an independent state of their own. If you consider Ukraine's population and the country's economic potential, the potential for growth and trade, you are looking at a new and important country in Europe, one that is larger than France, with a population over 50 million, with a substantial mainly agricultural resource base, and a well educated population. And yet it is a very young state and one which feels very insecure today about its national identity and sovereignty.

The one factor that will prove to complicate the post communist transition of the former Soviet bloc is what I call the "lack of maturity" of those states. I think every newly independent country in Europe will require some time before it learns how to operate in the new environment, how to compromise, how to cooperate with others and take less than the absolute maximum. In the case of the East European successor states after the First World War, it took two generations to learn international politics. The Soviet successor states have a long road to travel in that respect. Right now, the Ukrainians appear more concerned with the legacy of discrimination by the Soviet Union than with what we would consider vital economic and political concerns.

Q: Should we be concerned about the proliferation of the Soviet Union's nuclear weapons in light of the fact that the state is in disintegration?

A: Of course, for one simple reason: the assurances given by the Commonwealth governments are only as good as the governments that give them. Let me illustrate this point. Reportedly, a few weeks ago there was a test launch on an SS-18, one of the largest Soviet missiles, yet somehow we didn't know exactly where it occurred in Kazakhstan, and what was the purpose of the test. This is, needless to say, very disconcerting because it shows how tenuous the control mechanism appears to be. My basic argument is that obviously we cannot effectively preclude the proliferation from taking place, because it is taking place already. We know that Soviet nuclear engineers and technicians are being hired away from the former Soviet Union today by such developing countries as Libya, North Korea, and Syria, but I am not blaming those Russians for choosing a comfortable, warm Middle Eastern country, nice accommodations and a car over their present miserable existence in Russia. The question is, "Is this form of nuclear proliferation through the spread of nuclear know-how and technology a real threat?" It is a threat on the tactical weapons level, that is nuclear weapons are likely to figure ever more prominently in regional conflicts, especially in the Third World. On the other hand, from the point of view of the US, these weapons are unlikely to constitute a direct threat to our security. This is the kind of threat that can be now controlled by defensive systems, such as SDI.

In addition to nuclear proliferation, the proliferation of conventional weaponry is also taking place. The Russians have announced that they will sell conventional weapons, as have the East Europeans. For example, even though Czechoslovakia's President Havel announced in 1990 that Czechoslovakia would no longer supply weapons to the Third World and admitted that Czechoslovakia sold enough plastic to Libya to last Khadaffi for the next 10 years, two weeks later Czechoslovakia struck a deal to supply Syria with about 300 tanks, and then another deal to supply Nigeria with jet aircraft and small arms ammunition. We must recognize that the former communist states have no other alternative, because the military-industrial complex is such a vital part of their economies. Czechoslovak Foreign Minister Dienstbier defended his country's weapons deals saying, "We have 111 defense factories in Slovakia, and if we close them down, we see the end of our state essentially right before our eyes, because the Slovak separatists will use the loss of jobs as another argument for independence. So what are the alternatives?" In Russia there is also a powerful incentive to export weapons for hard currency. The defense industry is the only industry that can be described as "competitive," that is, the only industry that the Soviets can draw upon for foreign exchange earnings. In short, we are bound to see more and more conventional weapon systems offered for sale on the international arms market.

Focus on the 90's:
Economics at Home, Turmoil Abroad

Introduction of

L. William Seidman
by Winton M. Blount
Chairman of the Board, Blount, Inc.
Chairman of the Board, Rhodes College

It is an honor to introduce our distinguished speaker tonight. Our friendship goes back to the 1970's to the time when we were both involved in government. It was then that I came to appreciate Bill's no-nonsense approach to his responsibilities and to his penchant for "telling it like it is"... an attribute we don't run across too frequently in the world of politics.

Then, of course, Bill happens to be the nephew of two other important Seidmans: M.L. who is memorialized by this Lecture Series, and our good friend, P.K. who makes this Series possible.

Most of the world knows Bill as the former chairman of the Federal Deposit Insurance Corporation, a position he filled with distinction from October of 1985 until just recently... six years that would certainly try most men's souls. Bill was tested in the toughest arena in the world and they never laid a glove on him.

But Bill is also an accomplished businessman and a respected educator. Prior to this appointment to the FDIC, he was completing his third year as Dean of the College of Business at Arizona State University. While in Arizona, he was Chairman of the Governor's Commission on Interstate Banking and developed a proposal to open Arizona to full interstate banking. As an educator, prior to Arizona State, he is known as the "father of Grand Valley State University" in Allendale, Michigan, a state university with 12,000 students. He is also the founder of The Washington Campus, a consortium of 15 universities organized to help students and corporate executives understand the operations of the White House. (Now, how's that for a challenge!)

In business, Bill was managing partner of Seidman and Seidman, now know as BDO/Seidman. Under his leadership the firm grew from a small family enterprise to become one of the major accounting firms in the nation. He also served as Vice Chairman, Chief Financial Officer and Director of the Phelps Dodge Corporation. He has been a member of the Boards of Prudential-Bache Funds, Catalyst Energy Development Corporation, the Conference Board and United Bancorp of Arizona.

In addition to his recent position in government, Bill was President Gerald Ford's Assistant for Economic Affairs and served in similar positions in his native state of Michigan.

Bill holds the B.A. degree from Dartmouth College where he was elected to Phi Beta Kappa and the M.B.A. from University of Michigan where he was an honors graduate. But I am told that of all his claims to fame none is closer to his heart than his wife, Sally, his 6 children and his 10 grandchildren.

Ladies and Gentlemen, it is my great pleasure to introduce The Honorable L. William Seidman.

Focus on the 90's:
Economics at Home, Turmoil Abroad

Lecture Number Two by

L. William Seidman

Former Chairman,
Federal Deposit Insurance Corporation

Good evening, ladies and gentlemen. It's a pleasure to be here in Memphis to participate in the Seidman Town Hall lecture program.

It is a particular honor to be speaking at the M.L. Seidman Town Hall Lecture Series—M.L. was my uncle, a wonderful man whose interests are particularly reflected in this series.

I also want to pay tribute to P.K. Seidman, the junior brother and Mr. Memphis to me, who sponsored this series in M.L.'s honor.

I always revered P.K. as a great man and my "good uncle" because he was always a friend and counselor to his young nephew.

As I'm sure you all know, today is the day for wearing the green... which means that any speaker worth his salt must make some mention of St. Patrick.

But the problem is I don't really know that much about St. Patrick..... except that St. Patrick was called upon to cast the snakes out of Ireland.

My family had a similar experience in Grand Rapids.... And while a few of us wound up in Memphis, I had the misfortune of landing in Washington, D.C.

I enjoyed my years working in Washington—government service is one of most rewarding things a person can do—especially if you can get out of town without being indicted.

Right after I left the government I joined the press corps as the new business network, CNBC TV's Chief Commentator. This is quite a shift for me.

Just a few months ago I spent a lot of time and lung capacity complaining about my FDIC employees who leaked news stories to the press. Now I'm offering to buy a lunch for any and all who have a bit of news to impart.

My own DC experience illustrated how *dangerous* government

service can be. My office faced the White House grounds where the Presidential helicopters took off.

One of my first acts at the FDIC was to open the windows to let some fresh air in. The President's helicopter took off, and I was standing watching in awe. Suddenly, a helicopter gunship appeared at the window. And then two secret service guys broke in the doors and said, "Freeze."

A failed assassination plot. True story. Closest I came to really being shot down. From then on it was all a piece of cake. But I should have learned a valuable lesson. In Washington, you're best off if you keep your mouth and your window closed.

I'm pleased to be here, and have the chance to talk with you about our economy and the financial system of our country—particularly and especially in light of my recent tour of duty as FDIC-RTC Chairman.

I'll start with a little history, a history to provide the background of what I've called our current "balance sheet and restructuring recession." In the 80s, the greatest U.S. business heros were those who created the most debt.

The likes of Milken, Trump, Icahn and Keating were proclaimed as examples of great American business leadership—the kind that built our country. So every American, whether blue or red blooded, loved debt and abhorred those who thought it could be excessive.

Take Charles Keating. In 4 years he grew his institution from $600 million to $6 billion, all with funds from insured depositors, and almost all used for speculative real estate development.

I remember Keating giving a speech at the National Press Club. He was castigating me for complaining about the way he was increasing the debt load in the country. He recommended getting rid of me and putting Michael Milken in as Chairman of the FDIC.

I really agreed with that, Michael deserved retribution. But the eighth amendment of the constitution forbids cruel and unusual punishment, so it never came to be.

If you are in doubt about Milken's widespread illegal activities, read the book *Den of Thieves*. At the FDIC/RTC, I suggested we sue Milken because we had the evidence, as alleged in our law suit, that he illegally used the S&Ls to support his junk bond operations.

We stated in our complaint that he had cheated on his customers, his partners and his clients. We didn't say he created the S&L debacle or even a substantial part of it. We alleged that he was responsible for about 5 or 6 billion of the total $250 billion loss.

Milken hired Ms. Robinson (for a reputed $100,000 a month for PR), Harvard's Dershowitz and 4 big time New York law firms. We also hired a big league law firm to represent the government on a contingent basis—politically dangerous because our firm could make as much as $500 an hour if successful.

But we decided we would not play in the NFL of law suits with a high school team. The result: Milken's lawyers are willing to settle for $1.3 billion—a great day for the U.S. taxpayer.

Unfortunately, Milken will still be left with several hundred million. I'd hoped we'd only leave him with lunch money.

As I was saying, the 80s were the greatest debt binge in U.S. history, and that set the stage for the current recession. How big was the *debt problem* created in the 80s? While we were all aware that debt increased, I'm still amazed at the size of the increase between *1980 and 1990* and even more so when put in the context of coverage.

Aggregate US debt increased from $4 trillion in 1980 to $11 trillion in 1990, an increase from *1 1/2* times GNP to *2 times GNP*— or 33%. Home mortgage debt went up from 37% to 59% when compared to the value of the real property under mortgage.

Business debt went from 25% to 42% of stockholders' capital— again over 50%. Business cash flow to cover debt declined from 5.2 to 2.

Consumption, which had held steady near 63% of income for over thirty years, went up to 68%. As a result, savings went down from about 8% to 3%. It was self-evident that these kinds of increases could not continue. Live it up today and pay tomorrow always comes to a day of reckoning.

Herbert Hoover once said, "Blessed are the young, for they shall inherit the debt."

With all respect to President Hoover, he apparently never loaned his credit cards to his kids. I have. I know the last thing we need to leave our kids is debt. They are perfectly capable of creating their own.

I hate to quote speeches, even great ones, but I must quote from a speech which I gave over 5 years ago:

> At no time since World War II has the simultaneous growth of debt in both households and business sectors been so rapid. The current climb of debt in this country cannot be extended for many years. The rate of increase is just too steep. We must proceed with care. The flashing yellow caution light is operational.

The first part of that talk was exceptionally sound, but the last part, "The flashing yellow caution lights," was *awful*. I should have proclaimed, "The sirens are screaming and the red light is flashing."

The speech was made to banks and S&Ls that obviously were not listening to that kind of talk. The huge accumulations of debt continued.

My father always said, "We can't predict that the U.S. citizen will do, but we can predict that they will all do it at once." In this case, they were all going into debt.

Led by the S&Ls, much of the debt increase was fueled by financial institutions' lending—lending that has contributed greatly to the length of our current recession.

How did we ever get in the S&L mess - the mess that I call "The mother of all financial mistakes." The basic problem was the S&Ls were borrowing short and lending long—an inherently risky business.

The risk was revealed in the late 70s when interest rates rose to unprecedented double-digit heights. As the high rates persisted, the total interest *expense* of most S&Ls grew to exceed their total interest *income*; the S&L interest rate risk was revealed. As they say, "Only when the tide goes out do we discover who's swimming without a bathing suit".

The thrift industry was hurting bad, and, in the great American tradition, it went looking for relief in Washington.

The industry had long maintained a powerful lobbying presence in D.C. as well as a strong grass-roots network. So, what kind of medicine did the industry and the government prescribe?

First, generally accepted accounting principles were eliminated in favor of "regulatory" accounting standards that would allow insolvent thrifts to continue to operate. In effect, accounting gimmickry made lame and ailing S&Ls appear solvent.

For example, they allowed you to average capital over a 5-year period. This system assures you have some capital even if it has actually been zero for the last 4 years.

Then thrifts were given the power to diversify their investments into new ventures. No longer would they be restricted to home mortgages. Thanks to the Garn-St. Germain Act, the good old Bailey Building and Loan would never be the same.

Second, no supervision was provided or considered necessary to make sure the S&Ls used their new powers in a safe and sound manner. In fact, supervision of the S&Ls was reduced. The new law didn't require it, and the new Administration had no interest in providing it. The thrifts could use their new powers without government examiners looking over their backs.

Third, to sweeten the pot, deposit insurance had been increased from $40,000 to $100,000. This allowed practically unlimited access to funding—a $100,000 credit card from the U.S. taxpayers. Send the bill to Uncle Sam.

Crooks and highflyers had found the perfect vehicle for self-enrichment. Own your own money machine and use the product to make some highodds bets. We provided them with such perverse incentives that if I were asked to defend the S&L gang in court, I'd use the defense of entrapment.

The incentives of the game were just too attractive for some to resist.

But didn't anyone see the storm clouds on the horizon? Well, yes, there were a few prescient souls who made their concerns to the White House and to Congress.

Ed Gray, chief regulator of the S&Ls, a lover and not a fighter by nature, finally became a fierce advocate of increased supervision. And for his troubles, he gained the popularity of a bastard at the family reunion. Ed found out what Voltaire said was correct: "It is dangerous to be right in matters on which the established authorities are wrong."

Remember, this was the early days of the Reagan Revolution. And the battle cry of that revolution was "de-regulate now!" Anyone calling for more banking supervision was deemed a "re-regulator"—

a disloyal Reaganite.

In fact, when I decided the FDIC needed to meet the approaching problems of the banks by hiring more supervisors, I received my letter—"we cannot believe you have become a Re-regulator, etc."

Who were the individuals responsible for mixing the poisonous brew?

Alice Roosevelt Longworth said it first, "If you haven't got anything nice to say about anybody, come sit next to me."

We can begin with Chairman Richard Pratt, Ed Gray's predecessor at the Bank Board. Pratt and his board were the ones who changed the accounting procedures capital standards used by thrifts.

The Reagan years in the White House were heady times. Much good was accomplished. But sometimes the enthusiasm overrode caution. The enthusiasm to deregulate was a prime example and President Reagan's first Budget Director, David Stockman, definitely got carried away. He forgot that there are only two ways to discipline enterprises to appropriate behavior—market place economics or government regulation. In the S&L case, neither was present.

Maybe it was the certainty of youth. Or maybe it was the sureness of the ideologue. But Mr. Stockman had no patience for warnings that the Federal Home Loan Bank Board needed more supervisory resources to control the deregulated S&Ls.

The Administration was not entirely oblivious to the gathering storm clouds. Early in the decade the "Bush Task Force" was formed under the leadership of the Vice President to determine if the financial system needed reform.

Some good ideas came out of that study group... including one that would have required any S&L venturing outside the home loan area to convert to a bank charter and be regulated by much tougher bank supervisors. Unfortunately, the Task Force proposals were quickly crushed by S&L pressure groups.

But I don't want you to get the impression that the sole responsibility for not acting on the developing S&L crisis rested in the Executive Branch. Far from it. Congress gets a large share of the blame and for a variety of actions and non-actions.

Where to start. Perhaps we should begin with the Chairman of the House Banking committee, Henry Reuss, and the Chairman of the Senate Banking Committee, William Proxmire, and their part in 1980 in raising the deposit insurance limit from $ 40,000 to $100,000 per account at the behest of the S&L industry lobbyists.

Two years later, the Garn-St. Germain Act gave the thrifts the power to make loans and invest in risky ventures.

We should certainly mention departed House Speaker Jim Wright's holding hostage much needed S&L legislation as he strove to force regulators to act as he desired on problems concerning Texas thrifts.

Once it became known that there were problems in the industry, why did both parties remain silent? Well, the Republicans thought they were protecting de-regulations and the Democrats thought they were protecting their many fine constituent contributors in the S&L and housing industries.

It was what they call, in international nuclear war—MAD—Mutually Assured Destruction. The result of the S&L debt binge, a $200 billion plus bill to the taxpayer and a deep real estate recession, and a large government deficit.

Unfortunately the debt problem found the banks soon after the S&Ls. Their problems were different but they also primarily involved real estate lending encouraged by congressional changes in the laws. In 1982, in the name of deregulation, the Congress took out of the law, at the Administration's request, all the rules on construction and development.

Prior to that time there were specific rules about construction and development loans. The builder had to have a 25% equity. There had to be a "take out" and there were concentration limits.

At the same time as the regulatory rules were relaxed, new liberal tax incentives were provided for new real estate developments. There was a recession at the time and again "stimulating" the economy was in vogue.

Within fours years construction lending exploded—loans often made with no equity from developers—with banks providing upfront interest funding for the first three years of interest.

To slow this construction explosion, Congress removed the tax incentive in 1986 retroactively. As is so often the case, the remedy was worse than the malady. For example, by 1989, 9 out of the 10 largest banks in Texas failed or would have failed without rescue.

In each of the Texas banks, the principle cause of the problem were loans that would have been illegal before the law was changed in 1982.

When the Bank of New England failed shortly thereafter, the FDIC found the same illness. 80% of the loans that caused the failure were construction and development loans that could not have been made prior to 1982.

Banks were not traditionally large real estate lenders, unusually less than 10% of their portfolios was in real estate in the 70s. During the 80s this rose to 25%. Lack of a sound credit policy with respect to real estate loans was at the *heart* of the banking industry's problems.

As a result of the excesses in real estate lending the FDIC insurance fund needs refinancing. The banking problems have contributed to a reduced lending capacity, a disinclination to lend a balance sheet recession, and a credit crunch.

There were other areas of booming debt in the 90s: among them—consumer credit cards, junk bonds, and bank loans to developing countries.

Not the least of the debt aficionados was the federal government whose debt increased $1.7 trillion in the Reagan years. By comparison, in the prior 16 year period from President Johnson through Carter, the increase was less than $600 billion.

The annual increase in the Reagan years was about $211 billion. Unfortunately, in the Bush years, the yearly average has skyrocketed to $355 billion.

President Bush is correct, the budget was a mistake—perhaps because lip-reading proved to be unreliable, but more importantly because it didn't work to reduce federal deficits.

The result of the huge debt accumulated in the 80s is a long lasting recession—longer than any since the 30s.

Fed Chairman Greenspan said recently, "There is a deep seated concern out there I have not seen in my life time—in the context of an economy that is not all that bad."

Why is the recession so long and why are people so upset? Because this recession is different. Many of the job losses are the result of restructured of over-leveraged industries and are intended to be permanent—not layoffs until the recession is over.

Further, real GNP growth for the last 3 years is the lowest for any administration since World War II. A lower standard of living affects everyone.

In fact, the only other administration that comes close was the combination of Ford and Carter when we had the OPEC oil embargo and Watergate.

On election day, when the American people are asked, "Are you better off than you were 4 years ago," the majority will likely answer, "NO."

Do American people have a right to complain? Perhaps they don't since they participated in, and enjoyed creating the debts of the 80s. But this too, will pass!!

But there is the good news. The essentials for economic recovery are in place. Inflation and oil prices are down. Defense spending will get cut. Interest rates are low. Housing affordability is the best since 1974.

The spread in the yield curve is the widest in years. Nothing will strengthen our financial institutions faster than the low short rates and the higher long rates. The reduced cost of deposit goes straight to the bottom line.

Corporations and consumers are reducing their debt load and restructing their balance sheets. All the current numbers—retail sales, housing starts and sales, purchasing agents' index—even employment are looking up.

But the bad news is that it takes time to work our way out of the kind of debt we incurred.

How long do we have to wait for the return to better times? To be a recognized and acceptable economic expert today, it is mandatory to predict recovery within 6 months. All the best economic pros trained at our finest universities have been doing just that for the last 2 1/2 years.

How long this recovery will take and how strong it will be interests workers—white and blue collar—and all the Presidential candidates. We haven't had a recession like this recently.

Thus, studying past recessions is not likely to be enlightening. Everyday gives us new evidence, but today I'd say it's about even money the recovery will be just in time to save the Bush Presidency.

As we emerge from this recession, we will see major changes in our industries and financial institutions. Our manufacturing industries will be more competitive. They will be market niche oriented, cleaned up and productive. Our financial institutions also will be restructured.

New technologies will provide for paperless and at-home transactions, and TV interactive communications. Geographic regulatory limitations will decline nationally and internationally.

Different parts of the financial services industry have very different outlooks.

Banks will lose market share—the result of uncontrollable costs and limitations brought on by excess regulation.

For example, the 1991 banking legislation allows the regulators to set standards for executive compensation, internal control and risk management system. It requires mountains of new reports and imposes new social responsibilities in lending.

While more costs for banks are legislated, the opportunity to improve performance through supplying broader services and raising more capital from new social services was denied.

Further, the cost of deposit insurance is becoming prohibitive. Like any insurance fund, when there are too many sick, the well get sick trying to support the ill. Without cost effective deposit insurance, the future of a great many banks—particularly small and medium sized ones—is threatened .

Incidentally, it is obviously unfair for the banks to be paying for a government guarantee while their GSE competitors use Fanny Mae and are receiving their government guarantee for free. Another loss for the banks in their Washington battles.

Unless banks can beat back the regulatory onslaught, they will be the least vibrant part of the financial services industry. The leadership of the industry knows they must find a way to work together to change this outlook, but past attempts do not bode well for the future.

But as always, "When the going gets tough, the tough get going," and the best banks will do well despite the industry problems, and one of the most promising opportunities for income for the innovative bank will be fees for services.

The Savings and Loans, the big losers of the 80s, will be a

different industry in the 90s. While they, too, are heavily regulated, their portfolio restrictions actually were relaxed in the '91 bill. They have an increasing opportunity to become the national consumer banks of the 90s.

Of all financial institutions, S&Ls are helped the most by the current yield curve spread. Longer term and more important, they are operating in a cleaned-up industry.

The kinds of managers whose incompetence disrupted the industry and created high deposit insurance costs are gone. To improve an industry outlook, remove competitors who are on their way to failure.

Further, the S&L charter had advantages. The industry can raise capital anywhere—they're not restricted like the banks. They have just been allowed—assuming the regulations become final—to branch nationally. The S&L industry—yesterday's loser—is looking like a winner—but again only the biggest and best will provide above-average growth.

But the really fast growing part of the financial services industries will the the *"unregulated."* It is growing at over 3 to 4 times the rate of the regulated part of the industry.

I'm talking about big asset-based lenders like GE and ATT Capital and small loan-lenders like CIT and Household Finance, and mortgage bankers like Country Wide, equipment lenders, even pawn shops. The restrictions on regulated institutions open real opportunities for the nimble and innovative—free of burdensome government controls—to step in.

Over all, the financial services industry will emerge, stronger, more competitive and diversified, providing a sounder base for our economy.

I will conclude with a quick observation of the worldwide economic competition of the 90s. The US future economic success depends on our productivity and competitiveness.

The characteristics of a successful, competitive society will be knowledge, flexibility, innovation—no longer will natural resources, armies and size win the day.

Powershift by Toffler makes this point very well.

Innovative decentralized capital markets, leading-edge higher education and technology, and free enterprise incentives also will be the hallmarks of the best competitors. A mobile multi-racial citizenry will be an advantage.

I wrote a book about 5 years ago called *The American Advantage* which suggested that our system has those characteristics required for success in the 90s. It gave examples of the increasing productivity of America's manufacturing sector with the U.S. providing the leadership in many of the industries of tomorrow—software, biotech, aerospace and others. For example, Microsoft, a company that didn't exist 20 years ago, is worth more today than General Motors. More new companies are created in the United States each year than any two other countries in the world.

But we are not assured of success. We must deal with our social problems—problems of crime, K through 12 education, and the environment.

But our greatest challenge is to reduce our desire to have it *all* today, and fail to save enough to make tomorrow a better day. We can't eat our seed corn and burn our fence post for fire wood if we expect to have better days ahead. We need to save more and live within our income.

We need the leadership that's willing to make the hard decisions. Now I've been around Washington long enough to know that asking for hard decisions has been a good way to return to your hometown from the revered seat of power inside the beltway.

And I understand that the common belief that the way to get elected is to tell people that you've found a way for them to live better, while working less. Politicians call it a "long term quick fix". It may be that's the only way to get elected in this country. Do you really believe it? I don't.

The American people know what we need. Listen to a gentleman named Jack Guy, a 42-year old high school teacher in Columbus, Ohio:

> "We've gotten ourselves into the fix we're in because we've started living like our government", he said. "We spend too much, run up debt, drag out paying our bills, so one answer is to tighten up. Let's face it. We've got to scale back—not on our dreams, but on how we go about making them come true."

Not bad advice from the "people." Let's all pledge allegiance *this time* to a better future for our children and support those who will lead us in that direction.

Questions and Answers Following
MR. SEIDMAN'S LECTURE

Q: The higher, long term rate is good for the financial institution, but interest rates are higher than we would like to see them. Could you comment on that? And secondly, the demand for junk bonds is legal; we created the demands for junk bonds, in fact. Why were we so surprised that those who created the supply for junk bonds use all kinds of methods that are not good, but not unusual, in that type of environment. Could you comment on that?

A: With respect to your first point, the long term rates, which are now for Governments about 7 1/2 to 8%, are higher than we would like to see them. I agree with you - it is an ill wind that blows no good. All I'm saying is that the spread is impairing our financial institutions where the credit currency is. If the rates stay where they are and they're still reasonably low, then there will be a slow recovery. The rates are a reflection of the fact that everybody needs to restructure their balance sheets so that the demand-supply equation ends up with a higher number.

With regard to junk bonds, I don't have anything against junk bonds, I don't think they're wrong, illegal or even unwise. I simply object to people selling them in false markets using methods which are clearly illegal. I think junk bonds, properly sold, with people understanding the risks they are taking, are a perfectly sound way of financing and a way of investing for those who get a fair shake at knowing what is going on.

Q: What about savings and loans?

A: I don't think those are appropriate investments for savings and loans, and they are now forbidden to savings and loans. But they're okay for you if you want to take the risk. It is not any great mystery that the higher return you get, the more risk you are taking.

Q: Now that the Japanese economy is declining, what will happen to our economy?

A: The Japanese have cut back very sharply on the amount of U.S. debt they are buying. That is one of the reasons, in my view, why the rates are higher than you would normally see them at this time in a recession, and we will continue to pay somewhat higher rates. We got a tremendous boost from the Gulf War. We again became the safest place in the world to put money, and we have had a tremendous increase in people who want to use American debt as their safe harbor and to some extent that is offsetting a huge amount of Japanese funding that was coming in. The higher long term interest rates are, the slower the recovery will be. Where they are now is not going to choke off a recovery. It simply will make it slower than it would be if we could get them down to 6%. I can tell you from a long friendship and a working association with Alan Greenspan, the Chairman of the Fed, if he knew a way to get those long term rates down, he would push that button and get those rates down. He has no way to do it. If he lowers short term rates more, which he can do simply by buying out the market, he creates more funds and higher long term rates. Expect inflation to go up. I can tell you that Alan has searched his little black box there in the Fed and there is no button he found that he can push that will get long term rates down or he would have gotten them down to 6% where he would have liked to have seen them.

Q: I think I hear you saying that the federal debt has become uncontrollable. If that is so, what will happen if now, or some years in the future, we say 'well, we're going to repudiate that debt?'

A: I don't think that the federal debt is beyond control, but the line that it is on certainly will lead us to a place where it will be beyond control. In the history of governments, when their debt becomes unmanageable, they resort to inflation. I think the outcome of an unmanageable national debt is that you don't repudiate the debt, you simply print money to for pay it. And of course as you print, the money becomes worth less and less. So there is a great danger of debt becoming beyond that which we can handle with our economy and that we will have to print money to pay those debts and that will cause inflation, and we all know what inflation can do to productivity of an economy. That's why Alan Greenspan is so worried about doing anything more than getting rates down because he does have to print money to keep them down. When a Fed sets the short term rate of 3% it simply says, "We'll create whatever money is necessary to keep the rate there". So they are, in fact, always printing money. It has always amazed me that the greatest free marketeers in the world love the Fed in its controlling of interest rates, which is truly an intervention in the free market system to put it mildly.

Q: Why would the Fed currently be buying debt? Is not the effect going to be an increased interest rate?

A: Certainly if the Fed were buying debt in the amounts that would effect that rate it could have that effect. They have bought very little long term debt and really nothing that can effect a market place that is so huge that the Fed's action is not even a water cannon; its a squirt gun in an ocean. The amount of government debt that is exchanged everyday, in New York, runs between 500 billion and one trillion dollars a day, so that trying to handle that market by buying and selling really has minimal effect. I think that most of the actions that they have taken have been for temporary stabilization of the market, I don't think they have had any real effect on long term rates.

Q: Will you please comment on third world debt?

A: The news on the so-called LDC debt in the Latin American countries is pretty good. Most of those countries' economies are doing substantially better than they were in the 80's. Particularly Mexico, where we have seen them actually turn around and run a government surplus. Most of the lending banks have written down their LDC debt to current market which is generally in the area of 20 - 40% of face. The only one that does not have that debt written down to that level is City Corp. I don't think that debt is liable to endanger money-setter banks with the exception of City Corp.

Q: What is your opinion of how the RTC liquidation efforts are perceived and what opportunities do you see for a small person to cash in on that?

A: As some of you may know, I was the first chairman of the RTC; in fact, I was the first employee of the RTC. Three years ago they had one employee and one hundred billion in assets and it is now up to about 8,000 employees. Since, of course, I was the one who put them in business, I have difficultly giving you an unbiased report of how they have done. To put it in context, they have over about 700 S&Ls, with almost 400 billion in assets. They have sold about 220 billion of that 400 billion and they are starting to lay off people now. Because of this yield curve thing I talked about, the S&L cost is going to be less than estimated, the number of S&Ls that are going to fail are still huge - but are going to be less. Even the S&Ls that they own are doing better. So the RTC, I would say, is getting the job done. Not without a lot of mistakes, not without a tremendous amount of computer snafoos and other problems, but it is just a startup business. In the first two years, they sold 210 billion: does anyone else know a startup that is better than that? They lost 55 billion, of course.

With regard to buying assets, my successor, Al Casey, is a short time Postmaster General and long time head of American Airlines. He is a gentleman older than I am so he is determined to get this thing done swiftly. As he says, he doesn't even buy green bananas. They have programmed to sell 100 billion of their assets by September 30, and all I can say is if they do, there is going to be some tremendous bargains out there. So if you're looking for something, go to the RTC and find out what they have got in your category. They finally have their computer systems in shape so they might be able to tell you what they own, at least generally.

Q: Has the Federal Reserve already so monetized the debt that we are in for inflation just by what they have done?

A: Certainly inflation is not a near-term problem. If you look at the charts, I would say, they are safely on the side of not creating any major inflationary pressure. If they lower rates more, and if that doesn't bring us along in this recovery, then there certainly is that danger. Running the Fed is a tough job. It's almost as bad as the RTC and it lasts longer, but the fact is, given all of the stresses, I would give Greenspan pretty good marks; except he is acting a little late in getting started in bringing down interest rates. Given all that, and knowing the pressures there are, I would give my friend Alan pretty high marks.

Q: Regarding the shift of assets-lending from the depository institutions to the unregulated sector, will much of the Fed's control move that way?

A: That is a very good question. We're on ground that none of us really knows the answers in terms of what the financial system will be like and where most of the lending will be in unregulated industries. Of course, the creation of money will still be in the banking system, but I wish I knew the answer to that. I think the Fed is studying that very hard and I think they are well aware of the fact that this kind of development, if it goes on, could substantially change our understanding of how monetary policy works. Beyond that I really can't give you an answer. I think it is going to put us in a new era where it is much more difficult to control monetary policy, and since we live in an international monetary world now, it's even more difficult. I suppose there are some very bright young academics that are working very hard on that, and I know that the Feds are working hard, but I can't tell you where it is all going to come out. It is going to be different.

Q: Do you think there will be tax legislation to help the economy and if so, in your opinion, is that a viable way to help the economy?

A: I don't think that the tax legislation that is currently being bypassed by the Congress diagnoses properly what our problems are. It is designed to increase spending when we already have a consumer that is stretched out too thin and it follows the Keynesian view of recessions, which I don't believe is the proper analysis at this time. I would agree with Mr. Tsongas, and primarily with the President, that that is not what we need at this time, and besides which, it is really not big enough to make a great deal of difference. So I would hope the President does veto it and his veto is sustained.

Q: Do you think that this trend towards greater regulation for the banks should be reversed?

A: I think it has to be reversed; there are two sides to it. One is that they have loaded the banks with a huge amount of social obligations. Obligations to behave as though they were public utilities, when in fact they no longer are in a monopolistic position. I think they ought to get rid of that. These banks really ought to be under no more obligations to loan, except in what they think is good business, than any other businesses. That is not going to happen, but I think it would be nice if we moved in that direction. Even more importantly, we have to allow the banks to operate what I would call the "two window system". They can operate deposit-insured money if you go to this window in the bank, but if you want to invest in uninsured vehicles and the bank wants to be dealing in the kinds of loans which cannot be done inside an institution, there is a separate window for that. You get paid a higher rate at that window, they tattoo on your hand 'this is not insured' so you can't come back and claim that it was. The banks have to be given a broadened charter or they are simply not going to become relative in the kind of competitive world that we have.

Focus on the 90's:
Economics at Home, Turmoil Abroad

Introduction of

Georgie Anne Geyer

by Dr. Andrew Michta
Associate Professor,
International Studies Department, Rhodes College

I am honored to have been asked to introduce Ms. Georgie Anne Geyer as today's lecturer in the M.L. Seidman Memorial Town Hall Lecture Series at Rhodes College, but I am not sure she really needs an introduction.

She is known to many of us through her syndicated column on foreign policy and international affairs which appears three times a week in some 120 newspapers in the United States and Latin America, including *The Chicago Sun-Times, The Washington Times, The Seattle Times, The Denver Post, The Dallas Morning News, The Houston Post, Diario de las Americas,* not to mention our own *Commercial Appeal.* She is a regular guest on *Washington Week in Review* on PBS and a regular questioner on *Meet the Press;* she has appeared on the BBC, the Voice of America, and Inside Story, to name but a few.

Ms. Geyer's journalistic passion for getting the story led her to the mountains of Central America, where in 1966 she was the first American journalist to stay with and report on Central American guerrillas. In 1967 she went into Cambodia to interview Prince Sihanouk when all American reporters were forbidden from entering the country. In 1973 she went to Iraq and became the first foreigner ever to interview Saddam Hussein. There are many other examples of her dedication to survey the key events of our time. Ms. Geyer interviewed some of the most important international political figures, including US presidents, foreign dignitaries, and opinion makers. What makes her journalism unique is not only her sources, but the scope and perceptiveness of her analysis of international politics.

Ms. Geyer is not only an accomplished journalist. She is the author of several books, the most intriguing among them being *Buying the Night Flight,* her personal and political autobiography. Her other books include *The New Latins,* a comprehensive political, social, and cultural study of Latin America; *The New 100 Years' War,* which takes a closer look at the war-torn Middle East; and *The Young Russians,* a look at the new generation of Soviets coming up in the mid-1970's. In addition, Ms. Geyer has contributed chapters to a number of books on journalism.

Her career has been filled with excitement and often real danger. For example, in 1973 she was held by the Palestinians in Beirut who accused her of being an Israeli spy. Then in 1976 in Angola she was imprisoned for writing about the coup being prepared by the Minister of the Interior against the MPLA regime. Whatever the part of the world, Ms. Geyer would always go where the story was unfolding at the time.

Today, arguably, there is no more important story in international politics than the collapse of the Soviet bloc, the decomposition of the former Soviet Union, and the ongoing transformation of the Soviet successor states. This is a story that bears upon the future of the international system and upon America's place in it. And we should not be surprised to learn that Georgie Anne Geyer has just returned from a fact-finding trip to the Commonwealth of Independent States where she observed first hand the course of postcommunist reconstruction, with all its hope and dangers.

We are fortunate to have her here tonight to share with us her insights on the direction of change in the former Soviet empire. Ladies and Gentlemen, please welcome Ms. Georgie Anne Geyer.

Lecture Number Two by

Georgie Anne Geyer

Syndicated Columnist,
Universal Press Syndicate

Thank you very much. I am truly moved—and even a little stunned—at this wonderful reception in this wonderful city.

Ladies and gentlemen, let us ask tonight "the" question of our times: What happened? What happened in the last three years that we have seen the collapse of the Eastern superpower and changes that we never dreamed of from one end of the globe to the other?

Let me move into those questions obliquely, for the answers are not at all simple. When I first went to Latin America in 1964 as a foreign correspondent for the old Chicago Daily News, I was taken over by my first "little obsession." I thought that I was going to be bitten by the Chargas bug, a little-known but deadly bug that lives in the jungles of Brazil and the Andean countries. I had read about the Chargas bug, and much of my thinking about going to live in Latin America was dominated by the idea that I was going to be bit very quickly and die very quickly.

As a matter of fact, I never saw a Chargas bug at all.

Now, most of the time during the last 30 years, I held up pretty well, though covering the entire world. But about ten years ago, I wanted to go again to Central America for my column; and I became obsessed with the idea that, if I went to El Salvador, because the civil war was then at its height I was going to die in El Salvador. I thought this through a lot, and I thought, "Well, Gee Gee, if you think you are going to get killed in Salvador, don't go to Salvador!"

So I figured this all out with my little South Side of Chicago mind, and I advised myself, "Gee Gee, go to Nicaragua! Nobody's fighting there this week."

So I went through Salvador on the plane, and a lot of my journalist friends got out. The place seemed very, very quiet; and as a matter of fact, nothing happened in Salvador that week. I got to

Nicaragua and, going into the airport, I was third in line to go into
the main part— and at that moment somebody blew up the airport!

I thought that after all of that I had gotten over these little
obsessions, but in truth I had not. Another one faced me last
December and January, for I had decided to go and study some of
the republics in the Soviet Union the very winter when everything
was falling apart. But as I faced the winter, I now decided that, the
minute I got out of Moscow, I was going to die in a train or a plane,
or murderers were going to take my money and probably kill me.

So I got to Moscow for a week the second week of January, and
I had decided to take the train to Kazan out in historic Tatarstan,
which is directly East of Moscow, about fourteen hours by train.
Then I was going to return to Moscow by train and fly to the far East,
to the new nations of Kazakhstan, Kirgizstan, Uzbekistan, and
Azerbaijan.

Now I had the terror of the Chargas bug all revived and relived:
I decided in my tormented little psyche that the "train to Kazan"
would be the last word that the civilized world would ever hear of
me. And it got worse when I looked at the map and there was this
whole vast area of the Soviet Union and nobody, but nobody, was
out there. When the New York Times man in Moscow said, "Please
come back and tell us what is going on out there," that just reinforced
my old Chargas bug fears, because if the New York Times didn't
know, how was I going to know?

In short, I looked at the map and I saw darkness; I saw the last
unknown part of the world; and I focused on the train to Kazan
because I knew in my heart of hearts that it would be on that train
that I would draw my last breath.

But let me back up a few steps, before we go on—and I mean
s-t-e-p-p-e-s.

I had known Russia through long trips for the Chicago Daily
News in 1967 and 1971, and I appreciate Professor Michta
mentioning that time because I was doing research then on the young
generation in Russia. Indeed, I found out some most interesting
things, which led me to this trip and to what I found today. In those
earlier years, I would discover from sociologists and others that that
younger generation had no interest in ideology—that was 13th on
the list of their interests, according to the sociologists at the

University of Leningrad. What WERE the interests of youth in 1971: knowing the world, having a good job and family, having nice children, being able to travel...

It all turned out to be very, very different from what we were hearing about Russia, about this "ideology-driven" country. Indeed, I went in one day in Moscow to see the head of the Komsomol, the Communist youth organization, and he said in disgust: "We don't know if this generation would even fight for the country, it is so alienated."

Ladies and gentlemen, I was stunned with many of the things I found, and what I found was that there was an entire new generation which in the 1980s was to change the whole world. But my theories were very unpopular at the time, because no one wanted to believe that the Russians would ever change. (The book, "The Young Russians," probably sold all of 300 copies.) I further wrote that the adversary relationship between the U.S. and Russia was being vastly de-intensified and I said that it was probable that the competition between these two countries would develop to become a peaceful one and, given no wars and given a continuation of democratic ideals in the West, that the changes then occurring would intensify, continue and lead to an entire new world picture.

Well, that was sure a "bestseller!" But I am happy that, these many years later, I was right.

So it was that I packed up this winter for still another long trip to what had been the Soviet Union, to explore above all for myself and for my readers and for my own beloved country—what happened? How could this empire have collapsed so swiftly? How could this "Superpower" have ended in such an incredible morass? It took only two years, really, for two years ago they were still a superpower. And today the ruble is worth two-thirds of a cent and people are groveling for food.

I was, ladies and gentlemen, able to see something the world has never seen before: the collapse of an entire ideological and economic and military system without defeat in war.

I am deeply concerned about the psychological problems of the Russians and the former Soviets today. We see a profound sense of humiliation, terribly intensified because an entire people now must, in addition, adopt the ideology of its enemy—us—without a conquering army, and without being conquered in war, and at a time when their army was completely intact. The situation is made even worse by the fact that they have no idea of what really happened and no idea of how to do what they now must do, which is to somehow transform themselves (and their psychology and spirit) to Capitalist, free-market economies. They simply don't know what to do. Do you go to the corner and sell your precious things? Do you sell your body (literally) to foreigners you were taught for 75 years to hate? What do you do? What happened?

Let me start with Moscow. One of the first things that stunned me most this time was arriving at Sheremetyevo Airport and seeing Western signs all over the place. There's "American Express," there's "Baskin-Robbin's" Ice Cream," there's "Novotel..." It is all quite stunning, and one has to pause to wonder what all of this Western infiltration is doing to the psyches of the people, after, remember, being taught for 75 years that they alone had the ideology that would save the world.

The first afternoon, I went over to Red Square to get some air and there, in the corner of Gum's Department Store, directly in front of Lenin's Tomb, is a Christian Dior window. As I was wondering over this, I noticed that, in front of that window, was standing a young boy, very round-faced and about ten years old. Next to him stood a woman, taking money. And he was howling like a wolf.

At first, I thought from a distance that it was some Orthodox church chant. But when I got closer, it was all very, very strange. For at this point, a very well-dressed man—a Leonard Bernstein-type, very elegant and obviously cultured—walked up, fell to his knees before the howling boy, crossed himself, got up and gave money to the woman before walking away silently away.

I realized at that point, ladies and gentlemen, that I was seeing one of the legendary "holy fools" of Russian history; I realized how profoundly they were falling back into their ancient ways. When the "holy fools" of the Orthodox Church used to roam through the Russian forests, giving out howls such as this, people believed that society was so deranged that only the insane could tell the truth. Only—this was now occurring in front of the Christian Dior window of Gum's! It was at that moment that I began to think that I was really in an absolute mad place, in a madhouse, in an insane asylum which had been hidden from us behind the Iron Curtain.

I saw Ambassador Robert Strauss that week; and the first thing he said to me, with his ribald (and exact) Texas sense of humor, was, "You know, Georgie Anne, this place is just one son-of-a-bitch." Then five minutes later, he'd say again, "You know, Georgie Anne, this is just one son-of-a- bitch." He must have repeated that nine times in the hour I spent with him— and of course he was right. He also said to me, "Today the ruble market is worth $10 billion. The whole former Soviet Union is worth $10 billion. A wealthy man could come in and buy up the whole place!"

It was staggering; they were back where they were in 1945 as the war ended; only, Russians would tell me today that things were much more hopeless than in 1945 because then the war had ended and they had hope and they knew what to do.

So it was, at this time, that I prepared for the "train to Kazan." All week long, I was still dreading it, waiting for the feared Chargas bug to strike again.

Now, ladies and gentlemen, the romantic reason for ordinarily sane people doing odd things like climbing Mount Everest has long been "because it's there." Foreign correspondents, filled with the romance of it all, kept whispering hoarsely, "because it's there, because it's there," to explain their actions when someone asked— or did not. I paraphrase the reason for traveling through Central Asia in the winter of its defeat; my answer was "because it's—where?"

Actually, nobody really has enlivened many a cocktail hour or even a fermented mare's milk break with diverting chatter about Kazakhstan, Kirgizstan, Uzbekistan, Azerbaijan or Tatarstan, at least not since Marco Polo traipsed the Silk Road in the 13th century. But I was determined to go because no one was there and for other reasons that are still not really very clear to me. On the ground, I had the great benefit of working with the local Radio Liberty correspondents, so they would make the arrangements for me. This was invaluable; without them, the entire odyssey would have been impossible.

Well, as it turned out, the feared "train to Kazan" was just fine. As with the feared Chargas bug of olde, no highwaymen jumped out at me and nothing scared me at all. And after 14 hours, I was in the wonderful old city of Kazan, now the capital of Tatarstan, where the

Mongol hordes had come and where Ivan the Terrible had defeated the Tatars in 1552. I found that now, 440 years later, the Tatars were "getting even" with the hated Russians by having declared independence from the Russian federation. This was immensely important, because this was the first people still within Russia who were declaring their independence; this was the first break-up of historic Russia.

The first thing that hit me as I woke up the next morning on the train, before I got to Kazan, was that, instead of the old announcements about Soviet power, about Russia, about killing all the hated Yankee imperialists and defeating them in the world, the radio was talking about free markets and about Christian Democrat politicians visiting from Germany. As so many times on this strange voyage, I had to shake myself to awaken myself to these new realities.

And soon I was in Kazan, a beautiful old city with the white Kremlin of Ivan the Terrible brooding over the great Volga river, which meets the Kazanka and the Kama rivers at the confluence of Kazan. Here, too, there were beautiful Russian streets, with old wooden houses and 19th century mansions of the bourgeoisie, where Pushkin and Tolstoy had studied at the historic University of Kazan. I felt strangely at home, now that the "train to Kazan" was out of my life. I was truly in historic old Russia, and, with the ice and the snows, it was quite wonderful.

The first thing that surprised me was the fact that most people were just going about their average lives. People were working, they were trying, they were going to school, they were going to work. The situation was awful; but, I felt a certain comfort in that I felt a certain moral order— a natural moral order—in people. In the midst of this utter collapse and this utter degradation, they were going on. And I began to have my interviews. Everyone from the vice-president to people on the street averred absolutely to me that they were going to get out of the Russian Federation—they had already declared independence in August, 1990. They wanted to do it "peacefully," they wanted to do it in a "civilized" way. And Boris Yeltsin was not happy about this. He told them very early on sardonically to "get as much independence as you can!" Of course, only last week they had a referendum, and they voted again to get out of Russia—" getting even" after 440 years!

What they were trying to do to save themselves economically was interesting, if not very effective. They had started trying to develop "horizontal relationships" between the different former republics of the Soviet Union, in order to trade among themselves instead of everything going through Moscow, which they called the "black hole." But it wasn't working, and enterprise after enterprise was closing. Big enterprises! This was a rich republic, with huge defense industries and heavy trucks, and now people were living on salaries of $5 a month (from 500 to 600 rubles). But, as important as the economic problems were, I would soon see that the basic problem was a moral problem—an ethical problem—a psychological problem.

The former Minister of Education in Tatarstan explained the situation to me in these terms: "The psychology of people living in a planned society is that they are accustomed to work by decree, by the order that comes from above. Now we have 'market relations,' but nobody knows what that is. In the past, the government guaranteed the life of the person, so now people only wait. The individual now says, 'Now I have no workplace any more, and our big enterprises are closing...' You see, every enterprise was linked with thousands of others—from the Far West to the Far East—and now the country is totally divided."

After a few days, I got back on the "train from Kazan" and went back to Moscow—but by then I had lost my terrifying fear. So then I got on a plane and went out to the city of Alma-Ata, the capital of Kazakhstan. Now, this is one of the most incredible places I have ever seen, because this is where all of the economic experimentation in the former Soviet Union is taking place. Kazakhstan is the laboratory for economic change in the FSU. Kazakhstan is way up on top of the Chinese border, in Central Asia's Wild East. This is where businessmen from Houston to Seoul are doing everything but riding Mongol ponies and sending the Khans' couriers ahead to get dibs on Kazakhstan's "milk and honey"— read, oil and gold.

I was amazed at Alma-Ata, the city where a lot of Russian exiles had been sent by the czars and by Stalin. It is a beautiful city, with lots of parks, lots of snow and (one of the very nicest things) a wonderful hotel there that was built for the Central Committee of the Communist Party and now has to take the likes of us Western adventurers. So there I was, with the oil men from Houston and in effect anybody with the money and the madness to travel way out there.

I was rather amused, when I came home again, to find that the journalists who had gone with Secretary of State Jim Baker had said to me, "Wow, those hotels in Alma-Ata were really terrible." I said, "Oh, you didn't stay at the Dostyk, the old Central Committee hotel?" And he said, "There was a Central Committee hotel?"

So, yes, I did get a kind of perverse little kick out of that: that Baker's trip didn't know about the one good hotel in Central Asia!

But then, before I came here tonight, someone said devilishly, "Well, maybe the State Department did know, and they put the journalists at the bad hotels!"

At any rate, the whole place was very nice, and there was a distinct and different sense of movement out there. In the Dostyk, there was even a FAX (the only one, incidentally, that I saw anywhere in Central Asia), and the young woman who ran it advised me with enthusiasm, "Oh, we have no trouble getting FAXes through to Washington—it's Moscow we can't get any FAXes through to!"

Indeed, that mood of enthusiasm—at least on the upper levels—was very much the mood all across Central Asia. They wanted people to come from all over the world, they wanted businessmen and people to invest and have faith in them, they wanted journalists and tourists. But there were problems.

What they didn't want to give themselves was security for investment or assurances that capital brought there would be respected and increased. For instance, the Kazakhs made a big contract with Chevron Oil Company two years ago; and this fall they just canceled it because they decided it wasn't preferential enough for them. So the problem is that no contracts hold, that there are no rules for investment, that in fact they don't know what Capitalism is all about. There are businessmen all over the place and they were looking, but nobody was buying, because there was nothing to buy yet and nothing palpable to invest in.

People are coming. Businessmen are coming, and swaggering adventurers, and frontier oilmen, but there were very, very few journalists like me. The second day I was there, I went to a press conference with Nursultan Nazakbayev, the president of Kazakhstan. I am sure you have seen his picture—I was amazed that he looked so much like the late Mayor Richard Daley of Chicago. (I am from the South Side of Chicago, so you will have to forgive me some of these little quirks of mine, but he really did.) Anyway, this is a very interesting man, because when he saw the Soviet Union falling apart in 1988, he went to South Korea, Singapore, China and Japan. He was looking for "what works," and he found out. When I interviewed him in Alma-Ata, he said, "We have to have a period of authoritarian rule first in order to put the economy in order; then we can have democracy." He came to this conclusion after studying Lee Kwan Yew's Singapore, South Korea and the others. I hate to say it, but I think he is right; but we will go into that a little bit later.

At any rate, Alma-Ata must be one of the strangest places in the world because it is still extremely poor but there are all these vigorous people out there trying to do things. There is the economics advisor to President Nazarbayev, an American of Korean descent, the brilliant economist Dr. Chang Young Bang, who hailed from San Francisco State College. I went to him in the beautiful old mansion of the bourgeoisie and we talked for about two hours about the economy. In addition, there are also former enterprise managers who are working out new ways of transforming the formerly Soviet-controlled Kazakh economy. These men have gotten together, and then they got $200 million together from local and foreign sources. Today they have their own controlling enterprises and they even have their own banks. But I would warn you —be careful of the banks should you ever find yourself in Kazakhstan and get in the mood for investing $5 million! Because they don't always give the money back.

So that presents another little problem—you have businessmen coming in and they are carrying $30,000 or $50,000 in cash in briefcases. Me? I had $3,000 around my waist, much of it in small dollar bills—in the end, I spent about $3,000 of it. At first, I was terrified (the "train to Kazan" syndrome again) that everybody was going to rob me. When that didn't happen I felt considerably more secure.

Then there are lots of Turks out there and lots of south Koreans, one coming in from the West and one from the East, the Turks in commerce and diplomacy, the South Koreans from the East. It was rather humorous, when I said to someone, "Gee, that's an odd combination—I wonder what they have to talk about." And this person said, "No, it's not odd at all. They get along just fine because they talk about how they fought the Korean war together".

If you don't believe that this is often an Alice in Wonderland world, consider this: Maxim's, the great French restaurant, is going to open a restaurant in Alma-Ata, and Benetton's is opening in Turkmenistan and Azerbaijan. They will, of course, cater to the foreigners. The whole thing is absolutely incredible.

As I moved across Central Asia, I began to think metaphorically—metaphysically—about what I was seeing; and I soon came to the metaphorical example of "snow." This was because I was really in the heart of winter—I arrived in Moscow January 10 and arrived back home February 13—and I was soon overcome by thinking of what winter had always meant for the Soviets. When I was in Egypt in the late '60s and early '70s, the Egyptian military men would laugh and say, "What would the Russians advise us? They would say that if our military endeavors didn't work, just 'Wait for winter!'" The Egyptians, not surprisingly thought that was a little bit odd.

And so I began to think of the "waiting for winter" metaphor in almost everything I did. Then, one day when I was walking around Alma-Ata in the snow, which was very pretty and sweet, snow that I haven't really seen since I was a child in Chicago (some years ago), I began to realize that this time was different: this time, they were "waiting for winter to end." For, all of the former republics of the Soviet Union now are new nations of and on their own. They all want above all an end to the old dependency on Moscow. They want an end to the oppression.

Everywhere I went, they would say things like, "Oh, Turkish Airlines is going to come in here—they are going to stop here and they will go on the Seoul and Singapore! And El-Al is going to come, and we are building a railroad to China! That was the good part—people were just terribly excited about being included in this new web of the world. There was concomitantly a tremendous sense of relief, because finally they didn't have to do everything through

Moscow (the "black hole," they call it) any more. I kept asking, however, "Where are the Soviet soldiers?" For they had not been pulled back to Moscow yet. And they would answer mysteriously, "There are 5,000 of them out there..." Or, "There are 10,000 up there..." Or, "The soldiers are there, but the officers have left..." It was, to put it mildly, a very strange moment.

To get to Alma-Ata was the simple part. You could still fly from Moscow, where there were still some ground crews and some form of maintenance. But from then on, transportation was little less than horrifically frightening. From Alma-Ata, for instance I drove with some of the local journalists to Kirgizstan, to its capital Bishkek. Now, this is the poorest place in the former Soviet Union and it is the poorest new republic, but it is a very sweet little place. It is the only one of the new nations where they have a really democratically-elected government, and the Kirgiz nomads had a definite historic democratic tradition.

But the hotel, ladies and gentlemen—I'm not finicky, having lived the way I have lived, but this was the worst place I have ever stayed in my life. About the first night, which was roughly two or three weeks into the trip, I simply decided that I would never be clean again. I said to myself, "Gee Gee, don't try, because you will never get clean again. Never!" Still, I tried to bathe by wearing scuffs and simply standing in the middle of the filthy tubs and pouring water over myself in the bitter cold. Then one morning, about 3 am., I was lying in bed—it was very cold, and I felt myself suddenly like some of the political exiles that the czars and Stalin had sent out to Kazakstan and Kirgizstan, who never ever went back—and I began to feel that God had really abandoned me. I felt I was going to die soon; it was preordained. It was so far away that one of our diplomats characterized it thusly: "this is not the end of the world, but you can see it from here."

But we survive—at least. And when I got up the next morning I did feel a little better. I didn't feel God was yet lurking around there, but I did begin to think that maybe, just maybe, I would still get out. Since I am a practical sort, I realized that since I had got myself out there, I was going to have to get myself back. It was a lot easier to get there, I can tell you that, and I still go to sleep thinking I have that $3,000—which is what I carried—still around my waist for safety. When I dare to think about it all, it was really all pretty crazy.

But the trip was also touching. Take little Kirgizstan. It has only 4 million people, mostly Kirgiz tribesmen, and it sits atop the mountains of northern China. Only six percent of the land is valleys; all the rest is the snow-covered tip-tops of mountains that go right into the fabled Tien-Shan mountains of the legendary Silk Road of China. Ironically, the Kirgiz have the one really working democracy, and their president, Askar Akayev was a scientific worker in St. Petersburg for many, many years until he was called back a year ago and amazingly was elected president. He also has a very good team, and I was most impressed by him.

I spent quite a bit of time with him, and I asked him at one point why the Kirgiz were different from the other Central Asians? He answered, "Well, we are very pragmatic people, and we're very realistic. Alexander The Great came this way, and the Mongol Khans as well. The Kirgiz fighters, who were nomadic horseman, would fight with them for a while, but the minute they saw that they were losing, they would take off for the mountains, because they were a very realistic people and they didn't want to lose."

Personally, I thought that was great; these were the kind of people I like; I don't like people who are always fighting to the death— we've got quite enough of that in this world.

Then, the third day that I was in Bishkek, to my amazement and good luck, the first American Embassy in Central Asia was opened! I was naturally very thrilled by this. But I don't usually get as emotional as I did that day. I walked into the new embassy, which was a small grey house that had been used by the Komsomol or Communist Youth, and there was an old friend of mine, American Diplomat Edmund McWilliams, whom I had first met in Pakistan. I had seen him in Nicaragua only three months before, and he looked at me in some surprise and demanded to know: "Gee Gee, why are you following me?"

Of course, my guides just went crazy when they heard this, and I certainly went up in their estimation. When President Akayev also came that day and spoke in Russian, Kirgiz and English, it turned out to be a most touching ceremony.

Remember that this is a very grey and very colorless part of the world; and it is so poor, and so dirty, and everything is so grey, the sky is grey, the trees are grey; so that, when the American flag went up over this little embassy at the end of the world and the American national anthem was played and then the Kirgiz anthem was played, tears just ran down my cheeks. And that is not my usual manner of responding.

Then there was one funny little story that will always stay in my mind as most typical of Kirgizstan. The first night, we were moving into the hotel, I was so upset by this hotel that I lost my glasses. I had this cute but frivolous little translator named Nurilla, who had a pretty little Kirgiz face that always bordered on petulance, immediately pronounced: "Someone stole your glasses."

I said, "No, Nurilla, I lost the glasses." And I thought that the whole thing was past. Then, amazingly, we had an interview with the new democratic Minister of Interior. Now remember again, that less than a year ago in Kirgizstan, no one would have dared to talk to a foreigner, much less a foreign journalist. Now, instead, I am sitting with this charming young man, General Felix Kulov, who had stopped the hard-line Moscow coup of August from spreading to Kirgizstan (he arrested all the plotters). So, after an interesting hour with Kulov, we are walking out of his neat office and Nurilla said to me, "I told Kulov's men about your glasses."

I sighed. "Nurilla, why did you do that?" I asked. But I only shook my head in vexation and forgot it. because we were working 14 to 16 hours a day and I had other things to think about.

Anyway, we returned to the hotel that night about 8:30 p.m. and we went to my room, we're all exhausted, it is very cold and we are in this terrible hotel, and on top of all that there are these two great big guys standing menacingly in the hallway outside my door. At this point, the local journalist and Nurilla went to talk to these men, and my friends came back. "Who are they?" I demanded. And Nurilla said, smiling, "Why, they are Kulov's men! You don't have to be afraid now. They have questioned everybody in the hotel about your glasses."

As a matter of fact, I did feel rather secure after that. After that, every single person in the hotel knew who I was, and there was certainly not going to be any nonsense, not with "Kulov's men" around! But the great Odyssean saga of the glasses was not yet ended.

The morning I left, Nurilla suddenly got worried. She strode up to me in the lobby, just as we were leaving for the airport, and said to me, "You know, the hotel is very upset about the glasses." (I am thinking, meanwhile, "When is this girl going to leave me alone?") Then she added the astonishing, "They feel their reputation is at stake." (And I am thinking, "This hotel has a reputation?") And she said, "They fear that everyone is going to know that your glasses were stolen here—maybe you should say something to them?"

Finally, I said, more than a little irked, "Nurilla, I didn't say the glasses were stolen."

And she said, brightly, "That's right—I said that, didn't I?"

As we drove to the airport that day, I saw a very small but perhaps significant sign of the changes in that area taking place. One afternoon, Nurilla had pointed out to me the small, lonely, abused little houses of Bishkek, and mentioned how they had all had only one story under Communism, because "under Soviet power, no one would build a second story because that would show they had money— and then the Communists would clamp down on them." But as we drove to the airport, she said excitedly, "Look, there is a house with three stories!"

That was the day that I really took my life in my hands by flying on Aeroflot from Bishkek to Tashkent. Now, many of you have probably flown on Aeroflot in the past, and you probably think it was bad then. Well, today it is at least a thousand times worse. Going across Central Asia with Aeroflot is quite simply the worst and most dangerous thing I have ever done in my life. You must understand that the airports are closed. Basically, there is nobody there. They are filthy dirty. There are no ground crews, there's no maintenance. There are a lot of Aeroflot planes on the ground and they were being cannibalized for parts. You can buy tickets, but most of the times there are no planes that fly. Sometimes they would charge me in dollars, and then it would be $130-$170 a ride. If it was in rubles, it would cost about 75 cents. Once hanging precipitously in the air, you notice that the floors are filled with mud and water from the snow and urine from the toilets. But far worse than that was your fear that they were never going to land. Later, when I discovered that there were 36 unannounced crashes on Aeroflot last year, I had to say that, had I known that, I probably would not have taken the trip.

But I did get to Tashkent, the capital of Uzbekistan, and one day the local journalists and I drove down to legendary Samarkand, and there I got more than an idea of the fabled beauties of the buildings that the great and murderous leader, Tamerlane, built in the 13th century. We went into a modern building, and we were going to visit the new "stock market." As we sat with three Samarkand men, one said to me brightly, "There is our stock exchange, it is called Turkestan." And I said, "That's very nice." And he said, "There are 150 of us stockbrokers working here." And I asked, "Well, what do yo do?" I was genuinely interested.

But, as they explained it to me, it turned out that they were actually bartering goods, that it was not a stock exchange at all. I finally said, "What you are talking about is a commodities exchange, you are exchanging commodities." They agreed.

Then the first man said brightly, "You Americans should get in here very quickly. Who comes first will win!" I countered with, "What will we win?" He said, "We have lots of minerals." I asked what kind? At that, there was a blank look on all of their faces. That little scene came to me to be typical of everything I was seeing. They didn't have the faintest idea of any economic possibilities that the city or the region had. They were trying. They wanted to do something, but they just didn't know what.

Everywhere, too I found scenes of utter devastation of this ideology that has ruled these countries and these peoples for 70 some years. One type of devastation was the ecological destruction of the once-great Aral Sea. Indeed, I wrote in my column from Tashkent on the Aral Sea: "The threat to this vast crossroads of central Asia used to come from Moscow. It came palpably, in the form of autocratic orders, party bureaucrats and brutal security forces. Today probably the biggest threat to Uzbekistan's tentative, new, six months' independence is a strangely amorphous one. It came on the winds, carrying salt and poisoned dust as far South as the ancient city of Samarkand and even to Kigizstan on the Chinese border".

This new threat emerges directly from the death of the once-great Aral Sea. Until recent years the Aral was a vast, shallow 25,000-square mile oval-shaped sea, the world's fourth largest inland body of water. Today it is only a raw wound in the earth. As underwater mounds of salt and pesticides now open and begin to poison all of

Central Asia, the sea has become a Sahara, with ships marooned in what was the center. What I was told by all of the specialists there was that the poison dust is bring carried across the region, winters are becoming dangerously warmer, and all sorts of new diseases were spreading. Children around the seabed are being born with all sorts of deformities and abnormalities. It is, in short, one of the many, many devastating leftovers of Communism.

My next stop on this distinctly odd but fascinating trip was historic Baku, the capital of Azerbaijan which sits on the West side of the Caspian Sea. By that time, I was looking pretty bad. My practical and fashionable German lodencloth cape-coat was dirty and dragging; the red bandanna that I had sported so I did not look too foreign now made me look like a refugee. I knew it was time to get out when, three times as I tried to walk into my hotel in Baku, the Hotel Azerbaijan, the doorman would look at me and say, "Nyet, nyet, tolko inostrahnee!" Or, "No, no, only foreigners!"

I was naturally enraged, and I immediately blamed my coat and scarf for the fact that they thought I was a Russian. Instead, I abandoned my halting Russian and shouted in English, "I'm an American, I'm an American." I drew myself up as tall as I could, and then he let me in—but only hesitantly.

It was in Baku, too, that I saw the final fear that is just below the surface in all of the FSU and Central Asia and the Caucasus being realized. That is the threat, fear and now reality of the endless ethnic conflict being revived. In Baku, it is the conflict over the Armenian enclave of Nagorno-Karabakh between Armenia and Azerbaijan. Every day, while I was there and after, there were new devastations in the fight, new degradations, people being killed by having their scalps taken off. It was horrible and it will remain horrible and it is the realization of the terrible fear that, if economic development does not come soon, the failures of the whole societies will only finally dissolve into the atavistic ethnic fighting these peoples have known all of their histories.

But basically, we must get back to our first question—WHAT HAPPENED?

That was, of course, "the" question that I was asking myself, over and over and over, on this strange and I think rather symbolic trip.

Basically, I think that in the attempted transformation of the

Soviet Union, we are trying to do something that has never been done before. As my friend, Enders Wimbush, the director of Radio Liberty in Munich, puts it: "The real questions is this: Can a totally corrupt and valueless society, like the Soviet Union had become, somehow discover the spirit to transform itself through moral values, which are products of history and culture? Can those values be parachuted in effectively from outside?"

Far from idle questions, ladies and gentlemen, they are THE questions.

Before we get to the final question, which is that of the "Turkish airliner," let us focus on the astonishing fact that, in a period of basically only three years between 1988 and 1991, the entire powerful Soviet Union collapsed. So, what must come now for Russia and the new nations, so that they can recreate and recompose themselves modern nations? Finally are there any messages for us in that Soviet collapse?

When I try to go directly to the core reason the U.S.S.R. simply collapsed, I have to think it was because of a totally mistaken and flawed view of human nature. Soviet Communism saw human nature as spontaneously malleable. Through Communism, you could transform the human character and spirit overnight. I remember sitting in Kiev in 1971 with the head of the Chair of Scientific Communism at Kiev State University, one Dr. Kolobkow. He was a very nice, smart man, and he said to me, surely, "We will have the "new socialist man" in 1980. Partly being fey, I said, "What about 1981, or 1982...?" Seriously, he said, "No, 1980!" That was what Khrushchev said, too. It was strange, it was crazy, it was not backed up by any sense of any organic development of man.

Instead, it was mired in the firm belief that there was a revolutionary consciousness that must obey the dictates of the "scientific" Marxist ideology. All of that, of course, was under the control of the center, of Moscow, of the party. So, basically, I came up with the idea that Communism failed mostly because of this flawed idea of human nature and of the human person. They doggedly refused to see "man" as he is and the fact that what he really needs is a decent life and not ideological perfection assured through coercive utopianism.

It is not accidental that the United States became the world's first

totally "modern" country, or that that modernity and progress was
based upon morality. For the entire Capitalist system was based
originally on morality, on community and on the webs of bases of
trust that developed in the North of Europe several centuries ago.
The Protestant work ethic, the Hanseatic League, the guild system,
the apprentice programs, the banking system: it took 300 years,
beginning with the Protestant Reformation, and we still are far from
perfecting the Capitalist system, which is natural to us. Yet this is
what Russia and the new countries have to do today—they have to
do it in a very short time, without any time (or thought) to organic
development—and they have to do it without knowing what it is.
This came to me as what I really felt about this most extraordinary
situation that I was seeing. Then, on top of that, you put the fact that
in 1917 the Communists froze all those ethnic hatreds and conflicts
that had been there for centuries and now, with the freeze undone,
all of these hatreds are released by the new democracy without any
organic changes in those 70 years. I think we see what has happened.

One should add that it might all have turned out quite differently
had Mikhail Gorbachev begun to make slower but persistent
economic changes when he began perestroika and glasnost in 1985.
That would have given people—and the system—time to adapt.
Instead, by releasing political, intellectual and social energies first—
thus assuring the fact that the society no longer had the authority to
make the difficult economic transformation, or the power to keep the
conservatives from sabotaging it—Gorbachev literally made sure
that the whole process would be super-destructive to the system.
Gorbachev...was wrong; Kazakhstan's Nazarbahev is probably
right.

Are there any messages for us in this collapse? I think that there
are, and I would warn that, as wonderful and as great as this country
is, that there are things that we should be aware of that are warningly
similar to the Soviets' problems.

- We are trying to enforce a quality of outcome that is not
only impossible to obtain but which dooms the whole
society to mediocrity, which destroys prosperity and hope
for everyone. Again, it is a question of not seeing human
nature correctly.
- We are toying with the very idea of "group rights" that

they are trying desperately to get away from.

- We, like them, are giving impossible jobs to parts of our system, jobs that cannot be accomplished by the entity so assigned. If you need only one of many possible examples, consider the degree to which we are insisting upon giving parenting over to teachers, so that neither parenting nor teaching gets done.
- We are too often involved today in an incredible utopianism regarding language, so much so that we cannot even decide whether the international language of English should be our own official language.

One element of the strife all over the former Soviet Union that I have not yet spoken about is the question of language, which is everywhere. In almost all the new nations, they want to go back from the Cyrilic, imposed upon them by the Russians, to the Latin alphabet, if only so they can be part of the world. They desperately want to learn English, so they can be part of the bigger world, part of the world of business and intellect.

And in America, we cannot decide even if we want to make English our official language—or if we want, deliberately, to enter that world of endless conflict that are those countries split down the middle by language.

So, in the end, I also saw some of these similar problems that are in our age typical of all multinational and multi-ethnic societies, which are everywhere today dangerously fragile. If you want other cases, we have Yugoslavia breaking up, we have wars in the Caucasus and in Africa and militias and street gangs from Lebanon to Los Angeles.

(I was in the Gridiron Show in Washington this year, and we did a little act of our times called "Breaking up is hard to do." Each one of us was one of the former Soviet republics, breaking up.) And if you need still another example, consider India: a magnificent country, a culturally rich country, but one where the peripheries are breaking off: Kashmir, Assam, the Punjab. We are in a very difficult period of history for the basically artificial multi-ethnic countries, because they have always been fragile compared to societies which are societies of blood, of land, of shared history. I don't like that, but that is what I see.

Dr. Henry Kissinger recently summed up one of the strange conundrums of our own period of history at a meeting I attended, when he spoke to the question of what an extraordinary situation it is for a society like America to find itself in today. "I know of no society in history which has set out to do everything it finally did," he said. "But those exact qualities that led to our success from the previous period—the period of the Cold War— are perhaps not the qualities needed for the next period."

You will be happy to hear that I did get out. That is, I think you will be happy because otherwise I would not be here tonight. And that last day in Baku, after getting a dark feeling for the ethnic conflicts and the confusion and the uncertainty of where to go next, again I traveled to an airport filled with trepidation. I was going out on the one foreign flight a week—an amazing thing it itself for lands that have for so long been closed!—and I was to take the single Turkish Airlines flight on Monday evening to Istanbul, my favorite city in the world. And once again I was riven with still another little obsession, which was that the Turkish Airlines flight would not come that week. I was pretty tired by then, and as you already know I looked terrible; and the one idea that I absolutely dreaded was the idea that, if Mr. Turkish Airlines flight did not come, I would have to go back into Baku, I would have to try to get a ticket back to Moscow, I'd have to go through those two lousy airports, I'd have to go back to the Moscow hotel, I'd have to try to get a ticket out of Moscow... Your see why my spirits were low, when the very future of the world hung on the Turkish Airlines flight.

At any rate, at the airport, there was a whole bunch of us, and a lot of oil men because Amoco had that weekend signed a big deal with Azerbaijan for getting the rich oil under the Caspian Sea. We were all standing at the windows, with our noses literally pressed against the glass, our eyes futilely scanning the empty runways for our salvation. Hour after hour went by, and about 9 p.m (we were supposed to leave at 6 p.m.), wonder of wonders, the sacred Turkish airliner pulled into Baku airport. And I knew that I was back in the Western world, or almost.

Still, when we finally did get one, I still also felt I was in Russia, and I wasn't sure that this was all happening. Even when we got up in the air, I felt that, well, maybe we aren't going to Istanbul, maybe we are going somewhere else. Maybe we will go back. Then the hostess came by and she asked crisply, "What would you like?" And very suspiciously, because probably she was a Russian spy, I said, "I'd like two Scotch and sodas." And she said, "Fine what else would you like?" and I began, just began to think that maybe I really was getting out.

And soon you are going to get out too. But let me quickly go over my conclusions.

Where are we, what happened?

First of all, I think and know that the former Soviet Union can be transformed only through long-term value-laden, patient development, and through the veritable transformation of their institutions. Above all, it will need a kind of mutation or metamorphosis of their human nature. But how is that going to be accomplished?

My own feeling is that the plan that the Western nations made last week and that President Bush approved is basically about right; because it is not giving money and it's not pouring food in that will only be taken by the Russian Mafia. It is not pouring money in that we don't have anyway, but it is backing up the transformation of institutions through the World Bank and through the IMF. We need enterprise cores over there; we need businessmen to go and teach them; we need to bring many more of them here, and there are a lot of Russians already going outside. A thousand Russian students are in Finland now, and there are thousands of Central Asians, who have a Turkic language, going to Turkey.

Incidentally, Turkey is doing a wonderful job in the area, and Iran is coming in somewhat from the South; but the "great struggle" that you read about—that fundamentalist Iran and secular/Islamic Turkey are struggling for the ideological and religious heart of Central Asia is not true. These old/new peoples do not want to have a fanatic fundamentalist government, they want a Turkish blend of official secularism and personal religion. Most of them , after all, are only formally Muslim. In a city like Tashkent, for instance, there are two mosques.

I also met many American missionaries out of Alma-Ata, where there are approximately 100, not only American but South Koreans and others. They call themselves missionaries from the "moderning countries," and they are busy teaching needed skills like business English. There are Baptists there and there are Presbyterians, there are the South Koreans. They are really giving these societies what they need: moral techniques to modernization. There is also a missionary group called CINIM, which is largely American Protestant. They brought 300 Americans out to Alma-Ata last year for the big cultural festival, and they are sending no fewer than 600 Kazakhs to this country this year. All of this may seem small given the fact that there are 55 million people in Central Asia, but where else do you start? I think this is the place to start, because they cannot do it the way they are. It is not to denigrate their culture to say today that, if a people want to be a modern democratic and free enterprise country, they simply must have some of the values that underlie those systems and institutions.

The United States, meanwhile, must be terribly careful not to lose its own values having lost the external enemy as Henry Kissinger said. For our culture, too, has been weakened and changed by the long cultural struggle over individualism and collectivism in the Cold War. Enemies always devour something of the other. So we too need to turn inside and begin our own patient long-term tasks of rebuilding our education system, our highways, our infrastructure, and all without allowing ourselves to be divided into destructive special and self-interest groups which now truly threaten us. I am extremely happy to be here again. I am honored, I am thrilled by this wonderful audience, and I want to say again what a beautiful school you have here.

Finally, in closing, let me give you just a small personal precis of this extraordinary voyage which represented many things, above all the beginning of the end of the historic winters of dependency and of oppression of these historic peoples. Let me end with some brief personal notes:

For a quarter century, I have covered wars, revolutions, civil conflicts, street riots, and all; but then, some people say that, being from the South Side of Chicago, that's what feel I comfortable covering! Our mothers on the South Side were very nice ladies and they were very lady-like, but if some of these guys that I have covered around the world would have tried to walk down our street into our block, our mothers would have sent the dogs out.

But I have never experienced the bedeviling and complex world of devolution, of collapse, of breakdown that I saw this winter, where nothing holds people together from moment to moment except sheer willpower. I had never covered a world where "the answers" no longer exist through revolution because revolution is what got them where they were now. I had never contemplated societies where the ancient lessons of the storied Russian winter that I was sailing through were so fascinatingly clear.

I quickly perceived myself as a ship, with my trusty moneybelt, with my medicines, with my gauze (they don't have any in their hospitals anymore) and with my books and notebooks. I knew that if the ship kept going and didn't strike a torpedo or even a log that I would probably get out. But if the ship had any problems at all, I was in big trouble in these worlds without any backup or support.

But I was also sailing through that winter that the Russians and Central Asians used to endure simply by passively waiting—and I could see that the rules of those winters no longer applied. For everywhere I went, I met people who were trying, honestly and genuinely, to bring their peoples and little nations out of dependence and out of poverty and oppression. They knew that people must now take charge of modernizing their lives, or fail for all time—because this winter was the crucial moment.

In short, what I saw was terrible and wonderful. I was present at the freeze-frame moment of the collapse of an empire, and of the utopian ideology that had ruled these "subservient" peoples through terror. I was present at the first real moment of hope that these Central Asian and Russian and other peoples have had for centuries on end.

And that, my friends, was not a bad way to spend a winter.

Questions and Answers following
MS. GEYER'S LECTURE

Q: Have we just heard the outline of our newest book?
A: Well, I was thinking, frankly, of writing a little travel/literature genre book, a sort of classic travel book. I have so much more material describing the way it was this winter. But I don't know-Central Asia is a special taste. I don't know how many people are interested in it.

Q: I'm interested in finding out about Yeltsin, do you think he is going to last? And what about the Russian aid problem, didn't the German's put in a lot of money?

A: Well, those are good questions, I'm glad you asked because I didn't go into Moscow as much as I would have liked. I think personally, and I think this is instinctive, I think Yeltsin is going to last. And I think for various reasons, he is the first one who has grasped the fact that there have to be profound changes, and was willing to take the risk.

I became far less enamored of Mikhail Gorbachev on this trip very frankly. I took a lot of reading matter (you'd go crazy if you didn't take a lot of reading matter out there). I took a lot of magazines, a lot of books and I went through things and I would leave them. I read several books on the last 6 years of Gorbachev's period and everytime when he could have made changes that would have made it far less painful he pulled back and went back on the old hardliners. It is very clear now, even last August, he came out and said he still was an enthusiastic member of the Communist party. I became much more sympathetic towards Yeltsin and sympathetic to his anger at the end when he was left with the devastation of this collapsed empire and trying put it back together. I think he'll last because I don't think there are many who want the job. And we didn't get any feeling in Moscow about the military, although I happened to be there at that time when they all got up and berated Yeltsin, and Yeltsin tried to keep them in line. So you had a military that was extremely humiliated when I was in Berlin last

July. There were Russian Soviet soldiers selling their uniforms on the boulevards of East Berlin. This is a very dangerous type of thing, this kind of humiliation. But I haven't gotten any sense that the military really wants to take over.

On the aid problem, you're right, the Germans particularly put a lot of aid money, and I'd have to check the amounts, but a lot of it was just wasted because they sent food and they sent money. And that is why that is not the thing to do, I think this last program that was announced last week in which only 4 billion dollars will be American, that's a lot of money to me but it doesn't seem to be a lot of money to Washington. It was really going towards institution building and building up the international organizations. The IMF, for example, now makes it incumbent upon the Russians to continue their economic reform program. So to me that is the kind of aid that we should give - institution building. And I think on the personal level what is being done is backing that up and beginning the task of rebuilding the Russian mind, to bring it back to where it was in 1917 when they were beginning to build a slightly democratic but more capitalist society. And over and over the Russians said to me, "We're not 70 years behind, we're 200 years behind." And they are if not more.

Q: There is one point in your speech you mentioned that a reign of terror had kept down these ethnic rivalries since 1917, I wonder what the Czars did. It seems to me that they were pretty terrorist too, and whatever rivalries existed were suppressed in their days. One reason is, there must be at least 300 ethnic groups if you consider all of those different ones in Siberia. Can we anticipate that we will see the same type of violence as we are seeing between the Armenians and Azeris and the Georgians and Ossetians that don't like each other? Can you anticipate that?

A: What you are saying is very interesting, you're absolutely right. I just mentioned 1917 because I was talking about Soviet power. Everything you found in Communism was something as Nicholas Berkyaev, the great Orthodox philosopher, said was something you found under the Czar. Communism didn't come out of nowhere, it was a continuation of most of the qualities of the national state that you find under the Czar.

Let me just mention first that within the Russian federation, now Tatarstan has declared independence and took a referendum last week. The Western Siberians have a lot of secessionist tendencies and that would be a terrible loss to Russia—the whole Western Siberia. The Chechen-Ingush declared independence over a year ago and they are just sort of existing on their own in the middle of Russia; but it's small; it's not like Tatarstan. There are the Bashkiris, there are the Yacouts, all of whom are talking secession from the Russian federation.

Then we get down to where I was. I learned of ethnic conflicts, for instance, in Kirgizstan the border with Uzbekistan from 1989 or 1990, I'll have to check my notes, in a town called Osh, where the Uzbeks and the Kirgiz started to fight over land and 4 months later 1,000 people were killed. Never reported, because these places were never reported, no journalists were never allowed to go there, their Soviet press certainly didn't. So there are a lot of recent things there.

I think that the Caucasus is the cauldron. Georgia, Armenia, Azerbaijan... that's where the real horrendous fighting is going on and I don't see that kind of conflict in the rest of the country. I can see smaller conflicts but not fighting to the death. And I think that is really more a quality of historic Caucasus. The Georgians are fighting several peoples of the South Ossetians, and it is a terrible thing. There are journalists there reporting on it and I have to hand it to them, because I wasn't going to go there.

Q: Do you know if the United States, or any country in the world, could buy out all of Russia's weaponry, particularly all of the nuclear weapons right now so they won't be farmed out on the black market. Is there any likelihood that they will sell them all to us?

A: That's very interesting. I'm sorry to say I don't know. But I didn't really get into the weaponry thing. I was so involved more in the political and the economic changes. I talked to the Kazakh leaders about this and they were simply incomprehensible. I talked to Nazarbayev, and to the Vice-President, and in one breath they would say, "Well, we said we were going to give up all our nuclear weapons by 1994, didn't you know that?" And I'd say, "Well, I'd heard that." And two minutes later they'd say, "Well, no, we can't give them up until 8 years from now." It was simply impossible to figure it out.

I think the most honest man was an assistant to the Vice President in Kazakhstan, and I was talking to him before I went in to see Assanbayev, the Vice President. And this advisor said, "Oh, we are not going to give up our nuclear weapons because China still has territorial claims to us." And I said to myself, now that strikes me as the truth. They are not worried about what we're worried about, which is that the nuclear weapons are going to go up, they're worried that China is going to come and take some of their land.

So, that is not much of an answer but I didn't get into the overall bigger picture on that.

Q: In a column this morning, B.J. Cutler was saying that the 24 billion dollar aid package that is being sponsored by the administration to help the economy would be largely wasted. You probably know more about the Soviet Union than Mr. Cutler does. Do you agree with him?

A: I don't read other columnists. No sir, I don't mean to be smartass, I like B.J. very much, he is a terrific guy. But I don't agree with him on that. But I don't think anybody knows. Everybody I talked to, from Ambassador Strauss to the different Soviet people, I saw Jeffrey Sachs one morning in Moscow and he is the author of this whole thing. He confused me more than anybody but the one thing he said that I could understand was, "It's not working. This was 10 days after the economic shock and he said, "There should be food on the shelves and there isn't." I got so many different ideas. I don't think anybody knows what will work. But I do think that the West backing up international institutions who will go in there and take responsibility for themselves and will give Yeltsin and his reformers the message that the West is supporting him, I still think that is good. I can't make sense of the details and I'm no genius of economics, but I'm not that dumb. Everybody has a different idea. What I could see is that some things were taking root. These commodities exchanges (which they call stock exchanges) they are a kind of basic,

wholesale market, they're incipient, they're latent. There are things
that are beginning to take hold. I would disagree with B.J. on that,
but with all due respect, because he is a splendid journalist. And he
may know more about it than I do.

*Q: I have a question on the agriculture in the Soviet Union. Isn't
there a problem with the whole agriculture system?*

A: In every one of the Republics, I saw their Agricultural Minister
or one of his advisors and each place it was totally different. In
Kazakhastan, which is known for its nomadic horsemen and large
herds, they have no intention whatsoever of privatizing land. And
they say that the Kazakh people don't want it, which is probably true,
they're not small farmers. In Kirgizstan it was very different, they
wanted agricultural reform but every place I was these things were
just on the drawing board. I'd like to go back in a year, I think I'd
like to go back in a year - depending on how many years I have left.
I'd like to see if it took root. What they were telling me was from the
drawing board and I don't know if they are going to be able to put it
to work. Kergistan has 5% of land in valleys all the rest is in
mountaintops.

The one that would disprove what you are saying is Uzbekistan.
I think there were so many horrors of what the Soviets did to
themselves, to the Russian people, as well as to all of these
"subservient" peoples. Uzbeckistan was agriculturally, to me, the
worst. They diverted these two famous rivers to the north, they
diverted the water from the Aral Sea - all for cotton. They turned
Uzbekistan, which is one of the riches agricultural parts of the world
in a huge area which can grow everything, vegetables, melons, fruits
everything you want. They turned it, by order of Moscow, into
cotton - and cotton destroyed Uzbekistan. It destroyed the rivers. I
drove through from Tashkent to Samarkand, you could see the
irrigation ditches, they were just disasterous- they devastated the
land. In order to pick cotton they children from 4 years up going out
from school to pick it. Everybody there hates cotton.

In Hedrick Smith's book *The New Russians* which is a very good
book, one of the ones I read while going across, he tells the story of
the big cotton scandal in Uzbekistan when they sent a famous

prosecutor out from Moscow and he found the entire Communist party was corrupt and was skimming off all of the money from cotton. Rick Smith tells a story of Brezhnev and one of their drunken parties in Moscow and he is with the head of the Communist part from Uzbekistan and the head of the Communist party from Uzbekistan says, "We'll have 5 1/2 million tons of cotton and that will be our cotton quota." And Brezhnev says, "No, make it 6 million." And he says, "Okay, make it 6 million, let's have another drink." And that's the way everything was done. It is without any rationale, with any reason. And now you go down there and you find all of the waters are gone, cotton is a terrible crop, there land has been despoiled. I'd have to say that they feel that they don't really need a center, they certainly don't feel they need Moscow. Whether they will be able to do it is another question. What bewilders me is how they are even going to get back.

The final horror of the Aral Sea is that they have a fish preparation plant there which used to get fish from the Aral Sea. When the entire Sea dried up, because of this overuse of water for irrigation, they wanted to keep the fishing plant going. So even today they are bringing fish in from the Baltic countries to be prepared down there. So the mentality has not changed to a scientific agricultural mentality.

Friends of mine who are environmentalists who have gone down there say it has not changed. In fact, I asked them what's your answer about the Aral Sea which is a question about agriculture and cotton in Central Asia. And they say, "We're thinking about diverting water from the Caspian Sea." I thought, Oh my God, next year I'll come and the Caspian will be gone. The truly scientific mentally has not seeped in there yet.

Q: How does the rest of the world view the United States as far as benevolent Big Brother taking care of everything?

A: I came during the early years in Latin American covering Cuba, writing a book about Castro where everyone looked upon us as 'get the Americans out of here, don't let them get their imperialism out of there'. In Russian Central Asia they would love it if we would just take over. Literally, Russians said to me repetitively, "We wish that you had conquered us." I knew what they were saying, they were saying then we'd have somebody in charge.

This is another danger, and it's a danger with the Turks too. The Turks don't have the money to invest there and we don't either. The day I saw our embassy open in Bishkek, the capital of Kirgizstan, everyone was so hopeful- the President and all of his people were there and I had breakfast the next morning with our charge d'affaires, whose my old friend. He said, "The only problem is they don't realize that I have $7,500 to operate this embassy into the foreseeable future. Every dollar for our embassies in Central Asia has to come out of our Europeans embassies, so we have to close- not embassies- but portions in order to do it. This is going to be a big shock to them when they discover that far from not wanting us, they want us and we're not going to be able to do it."

We can hope that the big companies or small businessmen or Koreans can take up some of this slack. But America is still absolutely the hope to them. It's what they want to be, it's what they want a democracy to be, it's what they are studying- I mean, they're studying the federalist papers, they're studying the American constitution. Good luck.

Q: What has happened to Shevardnadze?

A: As far as I know he was back in Georgia last week or around that time. He is a very sane, intelligent man, I have a lot of respect for him. He could do a lot in helping Georgia, they have a lot of screwy ambitious men down there. I wish him luck, they need somebody like him to stop the fighting.